Frank J. Fabozzi, CFA
Yale School of Management

Sergio M. Focardi
The Intertek Group

Caroline Jonas
The Intertek Group

Challenges in Quantitative Equity Management

RESEARCH FOUNDATION

OF CFA INSTITUTE

Statement of Purpose

The Research Foundation of CFA Institute is a not-for-profit organization established to promote the development and dissemination of relevant research for investment practitioners worldwide.

ISBN 978-1-934667-21-7

11 April 2008

Editorial Staff

Elizabeth Collins
Book Editor

Nicole R. Robbins
Assistant Editor

Kara H. Morris
Production Manager

Lois Carrier
Production Specialist

Biographies

Frank J. Fabozzi, CFA, is professor in the practice of finance and Becton Fellow in the School of Management at Yale University and editor of the *Journal of Portfolio Management*. Prior to joining the Yale faculty, Professor Fabozzi was a visiting professor of finance in the Sloan School of Management at Massachusetts Institute of Technology. He is a fellow of the International Center for Finance at Yale University, is on the advisory council for the Department of Operations Research and Financial Engineering at Princeton University, and is an affiliated professor at the Institute of Statistics, Econometrics and Mathematical Finance at the University of Karlsruhe in Germany. Professor Fabozzi has authored and edited numerous books about finance. In 2002, he was inducted into the Fixed Income Analysts Society's Hall of Fame, and he is the recipient of the 2007 C. Stewart Sheppard Award from CFA Institute. Professor Fabozzi holds a doctorate in economics from the City University of New York.

Sergio M. Focardi is a founding partner of The Intertek Group, where he is a consultant and trainer on financial modeling. Mr. Focardi is on the editorial board of the *Journal of Portfolio Management* and has co-authored numerous articles and books, including the Research Foundation of CFA Institute monograph *Trends in Quantitative Finance* and the award-winning books *Financial Modeling of the Equity Market: CAPM to Cointegration* and *The Mathematics of Financial Modeling and Investment Management*. Most recently, Mr. Focardi co-authored *Financial Econometrics: From Basics to Advanced Modeling Techniques* and *Robust Portfolio Optimization and Management*. Mr. Focardi holds a degree in electronic engineering from the University of Genoa.

Caroline Jonas is a founding partner of The Intertek Group, where she is responsible for research projects. She is a co-author of various reports and articles on finance and technology and of the books *Modeling the Markets: New Theories and Techniques* and *Risk Management: Framework, Methods and Practice*. Ms. Jonas holds a BA from the University of Illinois at Urbana–Champaign.

Acknowledgments

The authors wish to thank all those who contributed to this book by sharing their experience and their views. We are also grateful to the Research Foundation of CFA Institute for funding this project and to Research Director Laurence B. Siegel for his encouragement and assistance.

Contents

This publication qualifies for 5 CE credits under the guidelines of the CFA Institute Continuing Education Program.

Foreword

Quantitative analysis, when it was first introduced, showed great promise for improving the performance of active equity managers. Traditional, fundamentally based managers had a long history of underperforming and charging high fees for doing so. A 1940 best-seller, *Where Are the Customers' Yachts?* by Fred Schwed, Jr., prefigured the performance measurement revolution of the 1960s and 1970s by pointing out that, although Wall Street tycoons were earning enough profit that they could buy yachts, their customers were not getting much for their money.[1] With few benchmarks and little performance measurement technology, it was difficult to make this charge stick. But after William Sharpe showed the world in 1963 how to calculate alpha and beta, and argued that only a positive alpha is worth an active management fee, underperformance by active equity managers became a serious issue, and a performance race was on.[2]

A key group of participants in this performance race were quantitative analysts, known as "quants." Quants, by and large, rejected fundamental analysis of securities in favor of statistical techniques aimed at identifying common factors in security returns. These quants emerged, mostly out of academia, during the generation following Sharpe's seminal work on the market model (see his 1963 paper in Note 2) and the capital asset pricing model (CAPM).[3] Because these models implied that any systematic beat-the-market technique would not work (the expected value of alpha in the CAPM being *zero*), fame and fortune would obviously accrue to anyone who could find an apparent violation of the CAPM's conclusions, or an "anomaly." Thus, armies of young professors set about trying to do just that. During the 1970s and 1980s, several thousand papers were published in which anomalies were proposed and tested. This flood of effort constituted what was almost certainly the greatest academic output on a single topic in the history of finance.

Quantitative equity management grew out of the work of these researchers and brought practitioners and academics together in the search for stock factors and characteristics that would beat the market on a risk-adjusted basis. With its emphasis on benchmarking, management of tracking error, mass production of investment insights by using computers to analyze financial data, attention to costs, and respect for finance theory, quant management promised to streamline and improve the investment process.

---

[1] *Where Are the Customers' Yachts? Or a Good Hard Look at Wall Street;* 2006 edition is available as part of Wiley Investment Classics.

[2] William F. Sharpe, "A Simplified Model for Portfolio Analysis," *Management Science*, vol. 9, no. 2 (January 1963):277–293.

[3] William F. Sharpe, "Capital Asset Prices: A Theory of Market Equilibrium under Conditions of Risk," *Journal of Finance*, vol. 19, no. 3 (September 1964):425–442.

Evolution produces differentiation over time, and today, a full generation after quants began to be a distinct population, they are a highly varied group of people. One can (tongue firmly planted in cheek) classify them into several categories.

Type I quants care about the scientific method and believe that the market model, the CAPM, and optimization are relevant to investment decision making. They dress in Ivy League–style suits, are employed as chief investment officers and even chief executives of financial institutions, and attend meetings of the Q-Group (as the Institute for Quantitative Research in Finance is informally known).

Type II quants actively manage stock (or other asset-class) portfolios by using factor models and security-level optimization. They tend to wear khakis and golf shirts and can be found at Chicago Quantitative Alliance meetings.

Type III quants work on the Wall Street sell side pricing exotic derivatives. They are comfortable in whatever is worn in a rocket propulsion laboratory. They attend meetings of the International Association of Financial Engineers.

In this book, Frank Fabozzi, Sergio Focardi, and Caroline Jonas focus on Type II quants. The authors have used survey methods and conversations with asset managers, investment consultants, fund-rating agencies, and consultants to the industry to find out what quants are doing to add value to equity portfolios and to ascertain the future prospects for quantitative equity management. This research effort comes at an opportune time because quant management has recently mushroomed to represent, for the first time in history, a respectable fraction of total active equity management and because in the second half of 2007 and early 2008, it has been facing its first widespread crisis—with many quantitative managers underperforming all at once and by large margins.

In particular, the authors seek to understand how a discipline that was designed to avoid the herd behavior of fundamental analysts wound up, in effect, creating its own brand of herd behavior. The authors begin by reporting the results of conversations in which asset managers and others were asked to define "quantitative equity management." They then address business issues that are raised by the use of quantitative techniques, such as economies versus diseconomies of scale, and follow that presentation with a discussion of implementation issues, in which they pay considerable attention to detailing the modeling processes quants are using.

The authors then ask why the performance of quantitatively managed funds began to fall apart in the summer of 2007. "Quants are all children of Fama and French," one respondent said, thereby providing a solid clue to the reason for the correlated underperformance: Most quants were value investors, and when market leadership turned away from value stocks, the relative performance of quantitatively managed funds suffered.[4] The authors conclude by addressing risk management and contemplating the future of quantitative equity management in light of the new challenges that have arisen in 2007–2008.

The survey-based approach taken by the authors has precedent in the Research Foundation monograph written by Fabozzi, Focardi, and Petter Kolm.[5] By asking market participants what they are thinking and doing, this approach elicits information that cannot be obtained by the more usual inferential methods. We are delighted that the authors have chosen to extend their method to the study of active equity management, and we are extremely pleased to present the resulting monograph.

Laurence B. Siegel
Research Director
Research Foundation of CFA Institute

---

[4]See Eugene F. Fama and Kenneth R. French, "Common Risk Factors in the Returns on Stocks and Bonds," *Journal of Financial Economics*, vol. 33, no. 1 (February 1993):3–56. Although this paper is not the first study to suggest that value investing is a superior strategy, it is the most influential one—or so the quote suggests.

[5] *Trends in Quantitative Finance* (Charlottesville, VA: Research Foundation of CFA Institute, 2006): available at www.cfapubs.org/toc/rf/2006/2006/2.

Preface

During the 2000–05 period, an increasing amount of equity assets in the United States and Europe flowed to funds managed quantitatively. Some research estimates that in that period, quantitative-based funds grew at twice the rate of all other funds. This accumulation of assets was driven by performance. But performance after 2005 deteriorated. The question for the future is whether the trend toward "quant" portfolio management will continue.

With that question in mind, in 2007, the Research Foundation of CFA Institute commissioned the authors to undertake research to reveal the trends in quantitative active equity investing. This book is the result. It is based on conversations with asset managers, investment consultants, fund-rating agencies, and consultants to the industry as well as survey responses from 31 asset managers. In total, we interviewed 12 asset managers and 8 consultants and fund-rating agencies. The survey results reflect the opinions and experience of 31 managers with a total of $2,194 trillion in equities under management.

Of the participating firms that are managed quantitatively, 42 percent of the participants reported that more than 90 percent of equities under management at their firms are managed quantitatively and at 22 percent of the participants, less than 5 percent of equities under management are managed quantitatively. The remaining 36 percent reported that more than 5 percent but less than 90 percent of equities under management at their firms are managed quantitatively. (In Chapter 1, we discuss what we mean by "quantitative" as opposed to "fundamental" active management.)

The home markets of participating firms are the United States (15) and Europe (16, of which 5 are in the British Isles and 11 are continental). About half (16 of 31) of the participating firms are among the largest asset managers in their countries.

Survey participants included chief investment officers of equities and heads of quantitative management and/or quantitative research.

1. Introduction

The objective of this book is to explore a number of questions related to active quantitative equity portfolio management—namely, the following:

1. Is quantitative equity investment management likely to increase in importance in the future? Underlying this question is the need to define what is meant by a quantitative investment management process.

2. Alternatively, because quantitative processes are being increasingly adopted by traditional managers, will we see a movement toward a hybrid management style that combines the advantages of judgmental and quantitative inputs? Or will differentiation between traditional judgmental and quantitative, model-driven processes continue, with the model-driven processes moving toward full automation?

3. How are model-driven investment strategies affecting market efficiency, price processes, and performance? Is the diffusion of model-based strategies responsible for performance decay? Will the effects eventually have an impact on the ability of all management processes, traditional as well as quantitative, to generate excess returns?

4. How are models performing in today's markets? Do we need to redefine performance? What strategies are quantitative managers likely to implement to improve performance?

5. Given the recent poor performance of many quantitative strategies, is investor demand for the strategies expected to hold up? If "quants" as a group cannot outperform traditional managers, what is their future in the industry?

As explained in the preface, we approached these questions by going directly to those involved in active quantitative equity management. They are our sources. We use the term "quantitative investment management" to refer to a broad range of implementation strategies in which computers and computational methods based on mathematical models are used to make investment decisions. During the 2000–05 period, an increasing amount of equity assets flowed to funds managed quantitatively. Indeed, some sources estimate that between 2000 and 2005, quant-based funds grew at twice the rate of all other funds. This accumulation of assets was driven by performance.

The question for the future is: Will the trend continue until the entire product design and production cycle have been automated, as has happened in a number of industries? In mechanical engineering, for example, the design of large artifacts, such as cars and airplanes, has been almost completely automated. The result is better designed products or products that could not have been designed without computational tools. In some other industries, such as pharmaceuticals, product design is only partially assisted by computer models—principally because the computational power required to run the algorithms exceeds the computational capabilities available in the research laboratories of even large companies.

Applying computer models to design products and services that require the modeling of human behavior has proved more problematic than applying models to tangible products. In addition to the intrinsic difficulty of mimicking the human decision-making process, difficulties include the representation of the herding phenomenon and the representation of rare or unique phenomena that cannot easily be learned from past experience. In such circumstances, do any compelling reasons favor the modeling of products?

Consider financial markets. Among the factors working in favor of modeling in finance in general and in asset management in particular is the sheer amount of information available to managers. The need to deal with large amounts of information and the advantage that can be obtained by processing this information calls for computers and computer models.

When computer-aided design (CAD) was introduced in the 1970s, however, mechanical designers objected that human experience and intuition were irreplaceable: The ability of a good designer to "touch and feel shapes" could not, it was argued, be translated into computer models. There was some truth in this objection (some hand-made industrial products remain all-time classics), but a key advantage of CAD was its ability to handle a complete cycle that included the design phase, structural analysis, and inputs to production. Because of the ability of computer-driven models to process a huge amount of information that cannot be processed by humans, these models allow the design cycle to be shortened, a greater variety of products—typically of higher quality—to be manufactured, and production and maintenance costs to be reduced.

These considerations are applicable to finance. The opening of financial markets in developing countries, a growing number of listed companies, increased trading volumes, new and complex investment vehicles, the availability of high-frequency (even "tick-by-tick") data, descriptive languages that allow analysts to automatically capture and analyze textual data, and finance theory itself with its concepts of the information ratio and the risk–return trade-off—all contribute to an explosion of information and options that no human can process. Although some economic and financial decision-making processes cannot be boiled down to mathematical models, our need to analyze huge amounts of information quickly and seamlessly is a powerful argument in favor of modeling.

The need to manage and process large amounts of data is relevant to all market participants, even a fundamental manager running a 30-stock portfolio. The reason is easy to see. To form a 30-stock portfolio, a manager must choose from a large universe of candidate stocks. Even after adopting various sector and style constraints, an asset manager must work with a universe of, say, three times as many stocks as the manager will eventually pick. Comparing balance sheet data while taking into account information that affects risk as well as expected return is a task that calls for modeling capability. Moreover, fundamental managers have traditionally based their reputations on the ability to analyze individual companies. In the post-Markowitz age of investment, however, no asset manager can afford to ignore the quantification of risk. Quantifying risk requires a minimum of statistical modeling capabilities. For example, just to compute the correlation coefficients of 90 stocks requires computing $90 \times 89/2 = 4,005$ numbers! Therefore, at least some quantification obtained through computer analysis is required to provide basic information on risk and a risk-informed screening of balance sheet data.

When we move toward sophisticated levels of econometric analysis—in particular, when we try to formulate quantitative forecasts of stocks in a large universe and construct optimized portfolios—other considerations arise. Models in science and industrial design are based on well-established laws. The progress of computerized modeling in science and industry in the past five decades resulted from the availability of low-cost, high-performance computing power and algorithms that provide good approximations to the fundamental physical laws of an existing and tested science. In these domains, models essentially manage data and perform computations prescribed by the theory.

In financial modeling and economics generally, the situation is quite different. These disciplines are not formalized, with mathematical laws empirically validated with a level of confidence comparable to the level of confidence in the physical sciences.[6] In practice, financial models are embodied in relatively simple mathematical relationships (linear regressions are the workhorse of financial modeling), in which the ratio of true information to noise (the signal-to-noise ratio) is small. Models in finance are not based on "laws of nature" but are estimated through a process of statistical learning guided by economic intuition. As a consequence, models must be continuously adapted and are subject to the risk that something in the economy will change abruptly or has simply been overlooked.

Computerized financial models are "mathematically opportunistic": They comprise a set of tools and techniques used to represent financial phenomena "locally"—that is, in a limited time window and with a high degree of uncertainty. When discussing the evolution of financial modeling—in particular, the prospect of a fully automated asset management process—one cannot take the simple view that technology is a linear process and that model performance can only improve.

---

[6]General equilibrium theories (GETs) play a central role in the "science" of finance, but unlike the laws of modern physics, GETs cannot be used to predict with accuracy the evolution of the systems (economies and markets in this case) that theory describes.

Some use of models may be helpful in almost any investment situation, but there is no theoretically compelling reason to believe that models will run the entirety of the investment management process. Although such an outcome might occur, decisions to use quantitative models in any particular situation (at least in the present theoretical context) will be motivated by a number of factors, such as the desire to reduce human biases or engineer more complex strategies. An objective of this monograph is to reveal the industry's perception of the factors working for and against modeling in equity investment management.

Does a "Best Balance" between Judgment and Models Exist?

On the one hand, the need to analyze a large amount of information is probably the most powerful argument in favor of modeling. On the other hand, a frequent observation is that human asset managers can add a type of knowledge that is difficult to incorporate in models. For example, it is not easy to code some judgmental processes, timely privileged information, or an early understanding of market changes that will be reflected in model estimates only much later. This difficulty leads some asset managers to question whether modeling is best used as a decision-support tool for human managers rather than being developed into a full-fledged automated system.

Models and judgment may be commingled in different ways, including the following:

- model oversight, in which the human manager intervenes only in limited instances, such as before large/complex trades;
- screening and other decision-support systems, in which models provide information to human managers, essentially narrowing the search and putting constraints on portfolio construction;
- incorporating human judgment in the models—for example, through Bayesian priors (see Chapter 2) or tilting risk parameters (that is, changing risk parameters according to judgmental evaluation of a manager);
- overriding models, in which the manager simply substitutes his or her own forecasts for the model's forecasts.

The key question is: Is one of these methods better than the others? Each of them has pitfalls. As we will see, opinions among participants in our study differ as to the advantage of commingling models and judgment and ways that it might be done.

Impact of Model-Driven Investment Strategies on Market Efficiency, Price Processes, and Performance

The classical view of financial markets holds that the relentless activity of market speculators makes markets efficient—hence, the absence of profit opportunities. This view formed the basis of academic thinking for several decades starting in the 1960s. Practitioners have long held the more pragmatic view, however, that a market formed by fallible human agents offers profit opportunities arising from the many small, residual imperfections that ultimately result in delayed or distorted responses to news.

Computer models are not subject to the same type of behavioral biases as humans. Computer-driven models do not have emotions and do not get tired. "They work relentlessly," a Swiss banker once commented. Nor do models make *occasional* mistakes, although if they are misspecified, they will make mistakes systematically.

As models gain broad diffusion and are made responsible for the management of a growing fraction of equity assets, one might ask what the impact of model-driven investment strategies will be on market efficiency, price processes, and performance. Intuition tells us that changes will occur. As one source remarked, "Models have definitely changed what's going on in markets." Because of the variety of modeling strategies, however, how these strategies will affect price processes is difficult to understand. Some strategies are based on reversion to the mean and realign prices; others are based on momentum and cause prices to diverge.

Two broad classes of models are in use in investment management—models that make explicit return forecasts and models that estimate risk, exposure to risk factors, and other basic quantities. Models that make return forecasts are key to defining an investment strategy and to portfolio construction; models that capture exposures to risk factors are key to managing portfolio risk (see the appendix, "Factor Models"). Note that, implicitly or explicitly, all models make forecasts. For example, a model that determines exposure to risk factors is useful insofar as it measures future exposure to risk factors. Changes in market processes come from both return-forecasting and risk models. Return-forecasting models have an immediate impact on markets through trading; risk models have a less immediate impact through asset allocation, risk budgeting, and other constraints.

Self-Referential, Adaptive Markets. Return-forecasting models are affected by the self-referential nature of markets, which is the conceptual basis of the classical notion of market efficiency. Price and return processes are ultimately determined by how investors evaluate and forecast markets. Forecasts influence investor behavior (hence, markets) because any forecast that allows one to earn a profit will be exploited. As agents exploit profit opportunities, those opportunities disappear, invalidating the forecasts themselves.[7] As a consequence, according to

---

[7]Self-referentiality is not limited to financial phenomena. Similar problems emerge whenever a forecast influences a course of action that affects the forecast itself. For example, if a person is told that he or she is likely to develop cancer if he or she continues to smoke and, as a consequence, stops smoking, the forecast also changes.

finance theory, one can make profitable forecasts only if the forecasts entail a corresponding amount of risk or if other market participants make mistakes (because either they do not recognize the profit opportunities or they think there is a profit opportunity when none exists).

Models that make risk estimations are not necessarily subject to the same self-referentiality. If someone forecasts an increase in risk, this forecast does not necessarily affect future risk. There is no simple link between the risk forecasts and the actions that these forecasts will induce. Actually, the forecasts might have the opposite effect. Some participants hold the view that the market turmoil of July–August 2007 sparked by the subprime mortgage crisis in the United States was made worse by risk forecasts that prompted a number of firms to rush to reduce risk by liquidating positions.

The concept of market efficiency was introduced some 40 years ago when assets were managed by individuals with little or no computer assistance. At that time, the issue was to understand whether markets were forecastable or not. The initial answer was: No, markets behave as random walks and are thus not forecastable. A more subtle analysis showed that markets could be both efficient and forecastable if subject to risk–return constraints.[8] Here is the reasoning. Investors have different capabilities in gathering and processing information, different risk appetites, and different biases in evaluating stocks and sectors.[9] The interaction of the broad variety of investors shapes the risk–return trade-off in markets. Thus, specific classes of investors may be able to take advantage of clientele effects even in efficient markets.[10]

The academic thinking on market efficiency has continued to evolve. Investment strategies are not static but change over time. Investors learn which strategies work well and progressively adopt them. In so doing, however, they progressively reduce the competitive advantage of the strategies. Lo (2004) proposed replacing the efficient market hypothesis with the "adaptive market hypothesis" (see the box titled "The Adaptive Market Hypothesis"). According to Lo, markets are adaptive structures in a state of continuous change. Profit opportunities disappear as agents learn, but they do not disappear immediately and can for a while be profitably exploited. In the meantime, new strategies are created, and together with them, new profit opportunities.

---

[8]Under the constraint of absence of arbitrage, prices are martingales after a change in probability measure. (A martingale is a stochastic process—that is, a sequence of random variables—such that the conditional expected value of an observation at some time t, given all the observations up to some earlier time s, is equal to the observation at that earlier time s.) See the original paper by LeRoy (1989) and the books by Magill and Quinzii (1996) and Duffie (2001).

[9]To cite the simplest of examples, a long-term bond is risky to a short-term investor and relatively safe for a long-term investor. Thus, even if the bond market is perfectly efficient, a long-term investor should overweight long-term bonds (relative to the capitalization of bonds available in the market).

[10]"Clientele effects" is a reference to the theory that a company's stock price will move as investors react to a tax, dividend, or other policy change affecting the company.

The Adaptive Market Hypothesis

The *efficient market hypothesis* (EMH) can be considered the reference theory on asset pricing. The essence of the EMH is logical, not empirical. In fact, the EMH says that returns cannot be forecasted because if they could be forecasted, investors would immediately exploit the profit opportunities revealed by those forecasts, thereby destroying the profit opportunities and invalidating the forecasts themselves.

The purely logical nature of the theory should be evident from the notion of "making forecasts": No human being can make sure forecasts. Humans have beliefs motivated by past experience but cannot have a sure knowledge of the future. Perfect forecasts, in a probabilistic sense, are called "rational expectations." Human beings do not have *rational* expectations, only expectations with bounded rationality.

Based on experience, practitioners know that people do not have a perfect crystal ball. People make mistakes. These mistakes result in mispricings (under- and overpricing) of stocks, which investors try to exploit under the assumption that the markets will correct these mispricings in the future, but in the meantime, the investor who discovered the mispricings will realize a gain.

The concept of "mispricing" is based on the notion that markets are rational (although we know that they are, at best, only boundedly rational), albeit with a delay. Mordecai Kurz (1994) of Stanford University (see the box in this chapter titled "Modeling Financial Crises") developed a competing *theory of rational beliefs*, meaning that beliefs are compatible with data. The theory of rational beliefs assumes that people might have heterogeneous beliefs that are all compatible with the data. A number of consequences flow from this hypothesis, such as the outcome of market crises.

Andrew Lo (2004) of the Massachusetts Institute of Technology developed yet another theory of markets, which he called the *adaptive market hypothesis* (AMH). The AMH assumes that at any moment, markets are forecastable and that investors develop strategies to exploit this forecastability. In so doing, they reduce the profitability of their strategies but create new patterns of prices and returns. In a sort of process of natural selection, other investors discover these newly formed patterns and exploit them.

Two points of difference between the AMH and the EMH are notable. First, the AMH assumes (whereas the EMH does not) that the action of investors does not eliminate forecastability but changes price patterns and opens new profit opportunities. Second, the AMH assumes (and the EMH does not) that these new opportunities will be discovered through a continuous process of trial and error.

That new opportunities will be discovered is particularly important. It is, in a sense, a meta-theory of how scientific discoveries are made in the domain of economics. There is an ongoing debate, especially in the artificial intelligence community, about whether the process of discovery can be automated. Since the pioneering work of Herbert Simon (winner of the 1978 Nobel Memorial Prize in Economic Sciences), many efforts have been made to automate problem solving in economics. The AMH assumes that markets will produce a stream of innovation under the impulse of the forces of natural selection.

The diffusion of forecasting models raises two important questions. First, do these models make markets more efficient or less efficient? Second, do markets adapt to forecasting models so that model performance decays and models need to be continuously adapted and changed? Both questions are related to the self-referentiality of markets, but the time scales are different. The adaptation of new strategies is a relatively long process that requires innovations, trials, and errors.

The empirical question regarding the changing nature of markets has received academic attention. For example, using empirical data for 1927–2005, Hwang and Rubesam (2007) argued that momentum phenomena disappeared during the 2000–05 period. Figelman (2007), however, analyzing the S&P 500 Index over the 1970–2004 period, found new evidence of momentum and reversal phenomena previously not described.

Khandani and Lo (2007) showed how in testing market behavior, the mean-reversion strategy they used lost profitability in the 12-year period of 1995–2007; it went from a high daily return of 1.35 percent in 1995 to a daily return of 0.45 percent in 2002 and of 0.13 percent in 2007.

"Good" Models, "Bad" Models. To paraphrase a source we interviewed: Any good model will make markets more efficient. Perhaps, then, the question of whether return-forecasting models will make markets more efficient is poorly posed. Perhaps the question should be asked for every class of forecasting model. Will any good model make markets more efficient?

A source at a large financial firm that has both fundamental and quantitative processes said, "The impact of models on markets and price processes is asymmetrical. [Technical], model-driven strategies have a worse impact than fundamental-driven strategies because the former are often based on trend following."

Consider price-momentum models, which use trend following. Clearly, they result in a sort of self-fulfilling prophecy: Momentum investors create additional momentum by bidding up or down the prices of momentum stocks. One source remarked, "When there is an information gap, momentum models are behind it. Momentum models exploit delayed market responses. It takes 12–24 months for a reversal to play out, while momentum plays out in 1, 3, 6, and 9 months. That is, reversals work on a longer horizon than momentum, and therefore, models based on reversals will not force efficiency."

Another source commented, "I believe that, overall, quants have brought greater efficiency to the market, but there are poor models out there that people get sucked into. Take momentum. I believe in earnings momentum, not in price momentum: It is a fool buying under the assumption that a bigger fool will buy in the future. Anyone who uses price momentum assumes that there will always be someone to take the asset off their hands—a fool's theory. Studies have shown how it is possible to get into a momentum-type market in which asset prices get bid up, with everyone on the collective belief wagon" (see the box titled "Modeling Financial Crises").

Modeling Financial Crises

During the 1980s debt crisis in the developing countries, Citicorp (now part of Citigroup) lost $1 billion in profits in one year and was sitting on $13 billion in loans that might never be paid back. The crisis was not forecasted by the bank's in-house economists. So, the newly appointed chief executive officer, John Reed, turned to researchers at the Santa Fe Institute in an attempt to find methods for making decisions in the face of risk and uncertainty. One of the avenues of investigation, led by economist W. Brian Arthur, was the study of complex systems (i.e., systems made up of many interacting agents; see Waldrop 1992). Researchers at Santa Fe as well as other research centers had discovered that highly complex global behavior could emerge from the interaction of single agents.

One of the characteristics of the behavior of complex systems is the emergence of inverse power law distributions. An inverse power law distribution has the form

$$F(x) = P(y > x) \propto x^{-\alpha}, 0 < \alpha,$$

which states that the probability that an observation exceeds x is proportional to x to the power $-\alpha$.

Power laws have interesting properties. In particular, in a power law distribution, the probability of extremely large events is much larger than it is in a Gaussian distribution.

The emergence of inverse power laws in complex systems suggested that financial crises could be interpreted in terms of properties of complex systems. Much effort was devoted at Santa Fe and elsewhere to understanding how fat tails are generated in complex systems. One possible explanation is the formation of large clusters of interconnected agents: In complex interacting systems, the distribution of the size of clusters of connected agents follows an inverse power law. Large networks of similar beliefs can be responsible for market bubbles. Another explanation is nonlinear dynamics: When processes are driven by nonlinearities, then fat tails and unpredictable chaotic dynamics appear.

The Santa Fe Institute effort to explain the economy as an interactive, evolving, complex system was a multidisciplinary effort involving physicists, mathematicians, computer scientists, and economists. Economists, however, had their own explanations of financial crises well before this effort. The maverick economist Hyman Minsky (1919–1996) believed that financial crises are endemic in unregulated capitalistic systems, and he devoted a great part of his research to understanding the recurrence of these crises.

According to Minsky (1986), the crisis mechanism is based on credit. In prosperous times, positive cash flows create speculative bubbles that lead to a credit bubble. It is followed by a crisis when debtors cannot repay their debts. Minsky attributed financial crises to, in the parlance of complex systems, the nonlinear dynamics of business cycles.

Stanford University economist Mordecai Kurz tackled the problem of financial crises from a different angle. The central idea of Kurz (1994) is that market participants have heterogeneous beliefs. He defines a belief as rational if it cannot be disproved by data. Many possible rational beliefs are compatible with the data, so rational beliefs can be heterogeneous. They are subject to a set of constraints, however, which Kurz developed in his theory of rational beliefs. Kurz was able to use his theory to explain the dynamics of market volatility and a number of market anomalies. He also showed how, in particular conditions, the heterogeneity of beliefs collapses, leading to the formation of bubbles and subsequent crises.

Nevertheless, the variety of models and modeling strategies have a risk–return trade-off that investors can profitably exploit. These profitable strategies will progressively lose profitability and be replaced by new strategies, starting a new cycle.

Speaking at the end of August 2007, one source said, "Any good investment process would make prices more accurate, but over the last three weeks, what we have learned from the newspapers is that the quant investors have strongly interfered with the price process. Because model-driven strategies allow broad diversification, taking many small bets, the temptation is to boost the returns of low-risk, low-return strategies using leverage." But, the source added, "any leverage process will put pressure on prices. What we saw was an unwinding at quant funds with similar positions."

Quantitative Processes and Price Discovery: Discovering Mispricings

The fundamental idea on which the active asset management industry is based is that of mispricing. The assumption is that each stock has a "fair price" and that this fair price can be discovered. A further assumption is that, for whatever reason, stock prices may be momentarily mispriced (i.e., prices may deviate from the fair prices) but that the market will reestablish the fair price. Asset managers try to outperform the market by identifying mispricings. Fundamental managers do so by analyzing financial statements and talking to corporate officers; quantitative managers do so by using computer models to capture the relationships between fundamental data and prices or the relationships between prices.

The basic problem underlying attempts to discover deviations from the "fair price" of securities is the difficulty in establishing just what a stock's fair price is. In a market economy, goods and services have no intrinsic value. The value of any product or service is the price that the market is willing to pay for it. The only constraint on pricing is the "principle of one price" or absence of arbitrage, which states that the same "thing" cannot be sold at different prices. A "fair price" is thus only a "relative fair price" that dictates the relative pricing of stocks. In absolute terms, stocks are priced by the law of supply and demand; there is nothing fair or unfair about a price.[11]

One source commented, "Quant management comes in many flavors and stripes, but it all boils down to using mathematical models to find mispricings to exploit, under the assumption that stock prices are mean reverting." Stocks are mispriced not in absolute terms but relative to each other and hence to a central market tendency. The difference is important. Academic studies have explored

---

[11] Discounted cash flow analysis yields a fair price, but it requires a discount factor as input. Ultimately, the discount factor is determined by supply and demand.

whether stocks are mean reverting toward a central exponential deterministic trend. This type of mean reversion has not been empirically found: Mean reversion is relative to the prevailing market conditions in each moment.

How then can stocks be mispriced? In most cases, stocks will be mispriced through a "random path"; that is, there is no systematic deviation from the mean and only the path back to fair prices can be exploited. In a number of cases, however, the *departure* from fair prices might also be exploited. Such is the case with price momentum, in which empirical studies have shown that stocks with the highest relative returns will continue to deliver relatively high returns.

One of the most powerful and systematic forces that produce mispricings is leverage. The use of leverage creates demand for assets as investors use the borrowed money to buy assets. Without entering into the complexities of the macroeconomics of the lending process underlying leveraging and shorting securities (where does the money come from? where does it go?), we can reasonably say that leveraging through borrowing boosts security prices (and deleveraging does the opposite), whereas leveraging through shorting increases the gap between the best and the worst performers (deleveraging does the opposite). See the box titled "Shorting, Leveraging, and Security Prices."

Model Performance Today: Do We Need to Redefine Performance?

The diffusion of computerized models in manufacturing has been driven by performance. The superior quality (and often the lower cost) of CAD products allowed companies using the technology to capture market share. In the automotive sector, Toyota is a prime example. But whereas the performance advantage can be measured quantitatively in most industrial applications, it is not so easy in asset management. Leaving aside the question of fees (which is not directly related to the investment decision-making process), good performance in asset management is defined as delivering high returns. Returns are probabilistic, however, and subject to uncertainty. So, performance must be viewed on a risk-adjusted basis.

People actually have different views on what defines "good" or "poor" performance. One view holds that good performance is an illusion, a random variable. Thus, the only reasonable investment strategy is to index. Another view is that good performance is the ability to properly optimize the active risk–active return trade-off so as to beat one's benchmark. A third view regards performance as good if positive absolute returns are produced regardless of market conditions.

The first view is that of classical finance theory, which states that one cannot beat the markets through active management but that long-term, equilibrium forecasts of asset class risk and return are possible. Thus, one can optimize the risk–return trade-off of a portfolio and implement an efficient asset allocation. An investor who subscribes to this theory will hold an index fund for each asset class and will rebalance to the efficient asset-class weights.

Shorting, Leveraging, and Security Prices

One of the issues that we asked participants in this study to comment on is the impact of quantitative management on market efficiency and price processes. Consider two tools frequently used in quantitative strategies—leverage and shorting.

Both shorting and leverage affect supply and demand in the financial markets; thus, they also affect security prices and market capitalizations. It is easy to see why. Borrowing expands the money supply and puts pressure on demand. Leverage also puts pressure on demand, but when shorting as a form of leverage is considered, the pressure may be in two different directions.

Consider leveraging stock portfolios. The simplest way to leverage is to borrow money to buy stocks. If the stocks earn a return higher than the interest cost of the borrowed money, the buyer makes a profit. If the stock returns are lower than the interest cost, the buyer realizes a loss. In principle, buying stocks with borrowed money puts pressure on demand and thus upward pressure on prices.

Short selling is a form of leverage. Short selling is the sale of a borrowed stock. In shorting stocks, an investor borrows stocks from a broker and sells them to other investors. The investor who shorts a stock commits to return the stock if asked to do so. The proceeds of the short sale are credited to the investor who borrowed the stock from a broker. Shorting is a form of leverage because it allows the sale of assets that are not owned. In itself, shorting creates downward pressure on market prices because it forces the sale of securities that the original owner did not intend to sell. Actually, shorting is a stronger form of leverage than simple borrowing. In fact, the proceeds of the short sale can be used to buy stocks. Thus, even after depositing a safety margin, a borrower can leverage the investments through shorting.

Consider someone who has $1 million to invest. She can buy $1 million worth of stocks and make a profit or loss proportional to $1 million. Alternatively, instead of investing the money simply to buy the stocks, she might use that money for buying and short selling, so $2 million of investments (long plus short) are made with only $1 million of capital; the investor has achieved 2-to-1 leverage simply by adding the short positions.

Now, add explicit leverage (borrowing). Suppose the broker asks for a 20 percent margin, effectively lending the investor $4 for each $1 of the investor's own capital. The investor can now control a much larger investment. If the investor uses the entire $1 million as margin deposit, she can short $5 million of stocks and purchase $5 million of stocks. Thus, by combining short selling with explicit leverage, the investor has leveraged the initial sum of $1 million to a market exposure of $10 million.

What is the market impact of such leveraging through short sales? In principle, this leverage creates *upward* price pressure on some stocks and *downward* price pressure on other stocks. Assuming that, in aggregate, the two effects canceled each other, which is typically *not* the case, the overall market level would not change but the prices of individual stocks would diverge. After a period of sustained leveraging, a sudden, massive deleveraging would provoke a convergence of prices—which is precisely what happened in July–August 2007. As many large funds deleveraged, an inversion occurred in the behavior that most models had predicted. This large effect did not have much immediate impact, however, on the market in aggregate.

The second is the view that prevails among most traditional active managers today and that is best described by Grinold and Kahn (2000). According to this view, the market is not efficient and profitable forecasts are possible—but not for everyone (because active management is still a zero-sum game). Moreover, the active bets reflecting the forecasts expose the portfolio to "active risk" over and above the risk of simply being exposed to the market. Note that this view does not imply that forecasts cannot be made. On the contrary, it requires that forecasts be correctly made but views them as subject to risk–return constraints. According to this view, the goal of active management is to beat the benchmark on a risk-adjusted (specifically, beta-adjusted) basis. The tricky part is: Given the limited amount of information we have, how can we know which active managers will make better forecasts in the future?

The third view, which asserts that investors should try to earn positive returns regardless of market conditions, involves a misunderstanding. The misunderstanding is that one can effectively implement market-neutral strategies—that is, realize a profit regardless of market conditions. A strategy that produces only positive returns regardless of market conditions is called an "arbitrage." Absence of arbitrage in financial markets is the basic tenet or starting point of finance theory. For example, following Black and Scholes (1973), the pricing of derivatives is based on constructing replicating portfolios under the strict assumption of the absence of arbitrage. Therefore, the belief that market-neutral strategies are possible undermines the pricing theory on which hundreds of trillions of dollars of derivatives trading is based!

Clearly, no strategy can produce only positive returns regardless of market conditions. So-called market-neutral strategies are risky strategies whose returns are said to be uncorrelated with market returns. Note that market-neutral strategies, however, are exposed to risk factors other than those to which long-only strategies are exposed. In particular, market-neutral strategies are sensitive to various types of market "spreads," such as value versus growth or corporate bonds versus government bonds. Although long-only strategies are sensitive to sudden market downturns, long–short strategies are sensitive to sudden inversions of market spreads. The markets experienced an example of a sharp inversion of spreads in July–August 2007 when many long–short funds experienced a sudden failure of their relative forecasts. Clearly, market neutrality implies that these new risk factors are uncorrelated with the risk factors of long-only strategies. Only an empirical investigation can ascertain whether or not this is the case.

Whatever view we hold on how efficient markets are and thus what risk–return trade-offs they offer, the measurement of performance is ultimately model based. We select a positive measurable characteristic—be it returns, positive returns, or alphas—and we correct the measurement with a risk estimate. The entire process is ultimately model dependent insofar as it captures performance against the background of a global market model.

For example, the discrimination between alpha and beta is based on the capital asset pricing model. If markets are driven by multiple factors, however, and the residual alpha is highly volatile, alpha and beta may be poor measures of performance. (See Hübner 2007 for a survey of performance measures and their applicability.) This consideration brings us to the question of model breakdown.

Performance and Model Breakdown. Do models break down? If they do, why? Is the eventuality of model breakdown part of performance evaluation? Fund-rating agencies evaluate performance irrespective of the underlying investment process; investment consultants look at the investment process to form an opinion on the sustainability of performance.

Empirically, every once in a while, assets managed with computer-driven models suffer major losses. Consider, for example, the high-profile failure of Long-Term Capital Management (LTCM) in 1998 and the similar failure of long–short funds in July–August 2007. As one source, referring to a few days in the first week of August 2007, said, "Models seemed not to be working." These failures received headline attention. Leaving aside for the moment the question of what exactly was the problem—the models or the leverage—at that time, blaming the models was clearly popular.

Perhaps the question of model breakdown should be reformulated:

- Are sudden and large losses such as those incurred by LTCM or by some quant funds in 2007 the result of modeling mistakes? Could the losses have been avoided with better forecasting and/or risk models?
- Alternatively, is every quantitative strategy that delivers high returns subject to high risks that can take the form of fat tails (see the box titled "Fat Tails")? In other words, are high-return strategies subject to small fluctuations in business-as-usual situations and devastating losses in the case of rare adverse events?
- Did asset managers know the risks they were running (and thus the possible large losses in the case of a rare event) or did they simply misunderstand (and/or misrepresent) the risks they were taking?

Fat Tails

Fat-tailed distributions make the occurrence of large events nonnegligible. In the aftermath of the events of July–August 2007, David Viniar, chief financial officer at Goldman Sachs, told *Financial Times* reporters, "We were seeing things that were 25-standard-deviation events, several days in a row" (see Tett and Gangahar 2007). The market turmoil was widely referred to as a "1 in a 100,000 years event." But was it really?

The crucial point is to distinguish between normal (Gaussian) and nonnormal (non-Gaussian) distributions. Introduced by the German mathematician Carl Friedrich Gauss in 1809, a "normal" distribution is a distribution of events that is the sum of many individual independent events. Drawing from a Gaussian distribution yields results that stay in a well-defined interval around the mean, so large deviations from the mean or expected outcome are unlikely.

If returns were truly independent and normally distributed, then the occurrence of a multisigma event would be highly unlikely. A multisigma event is an event formed by those outcomes that are larger than a given multiple of the standard deviation, generally represented by sigma, σ. For example, in terms of stock returns, a 6-sigma event is an event formed by all returns larger or smaller than 6 times the standard deviation of returns plus the mean. If a distribution is Gaussian, a 6-sigma event has a probability of approximately 0.000000002. So, if we are talking about daily returns, the 6-sigma event would mean that a daily return larger than 6 times the standard deviation of returns would occur, on average, twice in a million years.

If a phenomenon is better described by distributions other than Gaussian, however, a 6-sigma event might have a much higher probability. Nonnormal distributions apportion outcomes to the bulk of the distribution and to the tails in a different way from the way normal distributions apportion outcomes. That is, large events, those with outcomes in excess of 3 or 4 standard deviations, have a much higher probability in a nonnormal distribution than in a normal distribution and might happen not once every 100,000 years but every few years.

If the distribution is truly fat tailed, as in a Pareto distribution, we cannot even define a multisigma event because in such a distribution, the standard deviation is infinite; that is, the standard deviation of a sample grows without limits as new samples are added. (A Pareto distribution is an inverse power law distribution with $\alpha = 1$; that is, approximately, the fraction of returns that exceed x is inversely proportional to x.) A distinctive characteristic of "fat tailedness" is that one individual in the sample is as big as the sum of all other individuals. For example, if returns of a portfolio were truly Pareto distributed, the returns of the portfolio would be dominated by the largest return in the portfolio and diversification would not work.

We know that returns to equities are *neither* independent *nor* normally distributed. If they were, the sophisticated mean-reversion strategies of hedge funds would yield no positive return. The nonnormality of individual stock returns is important, but it cannot be the cause of large losses because no individual return can dominate a large, well-diversified portfolio. Individual returns exhibit correlations, cross-autocorrelations, and mean reversion, however, even though the level of individual autocorrelation is small. Hedge fund strategies exploit cross-autocorrelations and mean reversion. The level of correlation and the time to mean reversion are not time-invariant parameters. They change over time following laws similar to autoregressive conditional heteroscedasticity (ARCH) and generalized autoregressive conditional heteroscedasticity (GARCH). When combined in leveraged strategies, the changes of these parameters can produce fat tails that threaten the hedge fund strategies. For example, large market drops correlated with low liquidity can negatively affect highly leveraged hedge funds.

Risk management methods cannot predict events such as those of July–August 2007, but they can quantify the risk of their occurrence. As Khandani and Lo (2007) observed, it is somewhat disingenuous to claim that events such as those of midsummer 2007 were of the type that happens only once in 100,000 years. Today, risk management systems can alert managers that fat-tailed events *do* exist and *are* possible.

Nevertheless, the risk management systems can be improved. Khandani and Lo (2007) remarked that what happened was probably a liquidity crisis and suggested such improvements as new tools to measure the "connectedness" of markets. In addition, the systems probably need to observe quantities at the aggregate level, such as the global level of leverage in the economy, that presently are not considered.

A basic tenet of finance theory is that risk (uncertainty of returns) can be eliminated only if one is content with earning the risk-free rate that is available. In every other case, investors face a risk–return trade-off: High expected returns entail high risks. High risk means that there is a high probability of sizable losses or a small but not negligible probability of (very) large losses. These principles form the fundamental building blocks of finance theory; derivatives pricing is based on these principles.

Did the models break down in July–August 2007? Consider the following. Financial models are stochastic (i.e., probabilistic) models subject to error. Modelers make their best efforts to ensure that errors are small, independent, and normally distributed. Errors of this type are referred to as "white noise" or "Gaussian" errors. If a modeler is successful in rendering errors *truly* Gaussian, with small variance and also serially independent, the model should be safe.

However, this kind of success is generally not the case. Robert Engle and Clive Granger received the 2003 Nobel Memorial Prize in Economic Sciences partially for the discovery that model errors are heteroscedastic; that is, for extended periods, modeling errors are large and for other extended periods, modeling errors are small. Engle and Granger's autoregressive conditional heteroscedasticity (ARCH) models and generalized autoregressive conditional heteroscedasticity (GARCH) models capture this behavior; they do not make model errors smaller, but they predict whether errors will be large or small. The ARCH/GARCH modeling tools have been extended to cover the case of errors that have finite variance but are not normal.

A general belief is that not only do errors (i.e., variances) exhibit this pattern but so does the entire matrix of covariances. Consequently, we also expect correlations to exhibit the same pattern; that is, we expect periods of high correlation to be followed by periods of low correlation. Applying ARCH/GARCH models to covariances and correlations has proven to be difficult, however, because of the exceedingly large number of parameters that must be estimated. Drastic simplifications have been proposed, but these simplifications allow a modeler to capture only some of the heteroscedastic behavior of errors and covariances.

ARCH/GARCH models represent the heteroscedastic behavior of errors that we might call "reasonably benign"; that is, although errors and correlations vary, we can predict their increase with some accuracy. Extensive research has shown, however, that many more variables of interest in finance show fat tails (i.e., nonnegligible extreme events). The tails of a distribution represent the probability of "large" events—that is, events very different from the expectation (see the box titled "Fat Tails"). If the tails are thin, as in Gaussian bell-shaped distributions, large events are negligible; if the tails are heavy or fat, large events have a nonnegligible probability. Fat-tailed variables include returns, the size of bankruptcies, liquidity parameters that might assume infinite values, and the time one has to wait for mean reversion in complex strategies. In general, whenever there are nonlinearities, fat tails are also likely to be found.

Many models produce fat-tailed variables from normal noise, whereas other models that represent fat-tailed phenomena are subject to fat-tailed errors. A vast body of knowledge is now available about fat-tailed behavior of model variables and model errors (see Rachev, Menn, and Fabozzi 2005). If we assume that noise is small and Gaussian, predicting fat-tailed variables may be exceedingly difficult or even impossible.

The conclusion of this discussion is that what appears to be model breakdown may, in reality, be nothing more than the inevitable fat-tailed behavior of model errors. For example, predictive factor models of returns are based on the assumption that factors predict returns (see the appendix, "Factor Models"). This assumption is true in general but is subject to fat-tailed inversions. When correlations increase and a credit crunch propagates to financial markets populated by highly leveraged investors, factor behavior may reverse—as it did in July–August 2007.

Does this behavior of model errors represent a breakdown of factor models? Hardly so if one admits that factor models are subject to noise that might be fat tailed. Eliminating the tails from noise would be an exceedingly difficult exercise. One would need a model that can predict the shift from a normal regime to a more risky regime in which noise can be fat tailed. Whether the necessary data are available is problematic. For example, participants in this study admitted that they were surprised by the level of leverage present in the market in July–August 2007.

If the large losses at that time were not caused by outright mistakes in modeling returns or estimating risk, the question is: Was the risk underevaluated? miscommunicated? Later in this monograph, we will discuss what participants had to say on the subject. Here, we wish to make some comments about risk and its measurement.

Two decades of risk management have allowed modelers to refine risk management. The statistical estimation of risk has become a highly articulated discipline. We now know how to model the risk of instruments and portfolios from many different angles—including modeling the nonnormal behavior of many distributions—as long as we can estimate our models.

The estimation of the probability of large events is by nature highly uncertain. Actually, by extrapolating from known events, we try to estimate the probability of events that never happened in the past. How? The key statistical tool is extreme value theory (EVT). It is based on the surprising result that the distribution of extreme events belongs to a restricted family of theoretical extreme value distributions. Essentially, if we see that distributions do not decay as fast as they should under the assumption of a normal bell-shaped curve, we assume a more perverse distribution and we estimate it. Despite the power of EVT, much uncertainty remains in estimating the parameters of extreme value distributions and, in turn, the probability of extreme events. This condition may explain why so few asset managers use EVT. A 2006 study by the authors involving 39 asset managers in North America and Europe found that, whereas 97 percent of the participating firms used value at risk as a risk measure, only 6 percent (or 2 out of 38 firms) used EVT (see Fabozzi, Focardi, and Jonas 2007).

Still, some events are both too rare and too extreme either to be estimated through standard statistical methods or to be extrapolated from less extreme events, as EVT allows one to do. Nor do we have a meta-theory that allows one to predict these events.[12] In general, models break down because processes behave differently today from how they behaved in the past. We know that rare extreme events exist; we do not know how to predict them. And the assessment of the risk involved in these extreme events is highly subjective.

We can identify, however, areas in which the risk of catastrophic events is high. Khandani and Lo (2007) suggested that it was perhaps a bit "disingenuous" for highly sophisticated investors using state-of-the-art strategies to fail to understand that using six to eight times leverage just to outperform the competition might signal some form of market stress. The chief investment officer at one firm commented, "Everyone is greedy, and they have leveraged their strategies up to the eyeballs."

The Diffusion of Model-Based Equity Investment Processes

The introduction of new technologies typically creates resistance because these technologies pose a threat to existing skills. This reaction occurs despite the fact that the introduction of computerized processes has often created more jobs (albeit jobs requiring a different skill set) than it destroyed. Financial engineering itself opened whole new lines of business in finance. In asset management, the human factor in adoption (or resistance to it) is important because the stakes in terms of personal reward are high.

A major factor affecting the acceptance of model-based equity investment processes should be performance. Traditionally, asset managers have been rewarded because, whatever their methods of information gathering, they were credited with the ability to combine information and judgment in such a way as to make above-average investment decisions. We would like to know, however, whether above-average returns—from people or models—are the result of luck or skill. Clearly, if exceptional performance is the result of skill rather than luck, performance should be repeatable.

Evidence here is scant; few managers can be backtested for a period of time sufficiently long to demonstrate consistent superior performance. Model-based active equity investing is a relatively new discipline. We have performance data on perhaps 10 years of active quantitative investing, whereas we have comparable data on traditional investing for 50 years or more. Of course, we could backtest models

---

[12]A meta-theory is a theory of the theory. A familiar example is model averaging. Often, we have different competing models (i.e., theories) to explain some fact. To obtain a more robust result, we assign a probability to each model and average the results. The assignment of probabilities to models is a meta-theory.

for long periods, but these tests would be inconclusive because of the look-ahead bias involved. As we proceed through this book, the reader will see that many people believe model-driven funds do deliver better returns than people-driven funds and more consistently.

Sheer performance is not the only factor affecting the diffusion of models. As the survey results indicate, other factors are important. In the following chapters, we will discuss the industry's views on performance and these additional issues.

2. Quantitative Processes, Oversight, and Overlay

How did participants evaluate the issues set forth in Chapter 1 and other issues? In this chapter, we focus on the question: Is there an optimal balance between fundamental and quantitative investment management processes? First, we consider some definitions.

What Is a Quantitative Investment Management Process?

We call an investment process "fundamental" (or "traditional") if it is performed by a human asset manager using information and judgment, and we call the process "quantitative" if the value-added decisions are primarily based on quantitative outputs generated by computer-driven models following fixed rules. We refer to a process as being "hybrid" if it uses a combination of the two. An example of a hybrid would be a fundamental manager using a computer-driven stock-screening system to narrow his or her portfolio choices.

Many traditionally managed asset management firms now use some computer-based, statistical decision-support tools and do some risk modeling, so we asked quantitative managers how they distinguish their processes from traditional management processes. The variety of answers reflects the variety of implementations, which is not surprising because no financial model or quantitative process can be considered an implementation of an empirically validated theory. As one participant noted, quantitative modeling is more "problem solving" than science. Nevertheless, quantitative processes share a number of qualifying characteristics.

Asset managers, whether fundamental or quantitative, have a similar objective: to deliver returns to their clients. But they go about it differently, and the way they go about it allows the development of products with different characteristics. A source at a firm that uses fundamental and quantitative processes said, "Both fundamental managers and 'quants' start with an investment idea. In a fundamental process, the manager gets an idea and builds the portfolio by picking stocks one by one. A 'quant' will find data to test, test the data, identify alpha signals, and do portfolio construction with risk controls. Fundamental managers are the snipers; quants use a shot-gun approach."

The definitions we use, although quite common in the industry, could be misleading for two reasons. First, computerized investment management processes are not necessarily quantitative; some are based on sets of qualitative rules implemented through computer programs. Second, not all human investment processes are based on fundamental information. The most obvious example is technical analysis, which is based on the visual inspection of the shapes of price processes. In addition, many computer models are based largely on fundamental information. Among our sources, about 90 percent of the quantitative model is typically tilted toward fundamental factors, with technical factors (such as price or momentum) accounting for the rest.

More precise language would separate "judgmental" investment processes (i.e., processes in which decisions are made by humans using judgment and intuition or visual shape recognition) from "automated" (computer-driven) processes. "Fundamental" and "quantitative" are the commonly used terms, however, so we have used them.

A model-driven investment management process has three parts:

- the input system,
- the forecasting engine, and
- the portfolio construction engine.

The input system provides all the necessary input—data or rules. The forecasting engine provides the forecasts for prices, returns, and risk parameters. (Every investment management process, both fundamental and quantitative, is based on return forecasts.) In a model-driven process, forecasts are then fed to a portfolio construction engine, which might consist of an optimizer or a heuristics-based system. Heuristic rules are portfolio formation rules that have been suggested by experience and reasoning but are not completely formalized. For example, in a long–short fund, a heuristic for portfolio formation might be to go long a predetermined fraction of the stocks with the highest expected returns and to short a predetermined fraction of stocks with the lowest expected returns; to reduce turnover, the rule might also constrain the number of stocks that can be replaced at each trading date.

Investment management processes are characterized by how and when humans intervene and how the various components work. In principle, in a traditional process, the asset manager makes the decision at each step. In a quantitative approach, the degree of discretion a portfolio manager can exercise relative to the model will vary considerably from process to process. Asset managers coming from the passive management arena or academia, because they have long experience with models, typically keep the degree of a manager's discretion low. Asset managers who are starting out from a fundamental process typically allow a great deal of discretion, especially in times of rare market events.

The question, someone remarked, is: How quant are you? The head of quantitative investment at a large financial firm said, "The endgame of a quantitative process is to reflect fundamental insights and investment opinions with a model and never override the model."

Among participants in this study, two-thirds have model-driven processes that allow only minimum (5–10 percent) discretion or oversight. The oversight is typically to make sure that the numbers make sense and that buy orders are not issued for companies that are the subject of news or rumors not accounted for by the model. Model oversight is a control function. Also, oversight is typically exercised when large positions are involved. A head of quantitative equity said, "Decision making is 95 percent model driven, but we will look at a trader's list and do a sanity check to pull a trade if necessary."

A source at a firm with both fundamental and quant processes said, "Quants deal with a lot of stocks and get most things right, but some quants talk to fundamental analysts before every trade; others, only for their biggest trades or only where they know that there is something exogenous, such as management turmoil or production bottlenecks."

Some firms have automated the process of checking to see whether there are exogenous events that might affect the investment decisions. One source said, "Our process is model driven with about 5 percent oversight. We ask ourselves, 'Do the numbers make sense?' And we do news scanning and flagging using in-house software as well as software from a provider of business information."

Other sources mentioned using oversight in the case of rare events unfolding, such as those of July–August 2007. The head of quantitative management at a large firm said, "In situations of extreme market events, portfolio managers talk more to traders. We use Bayesian learning to learn from past events, but in general, dislocations in the market are hard to model." Bayesian priors are a disciplined way to integrate historical data and a manager's judgment into the model (see the box titled "Bayesian Statistics: Commingling Judgment and Statistics").

Bayesian Statistics: Commingling Judgment and Statistics

The fundamental uncertainty associated with any probability statement (see the box titled "Can Uncertainty Be Measured?") is the starting point of Bayesian statistics. Bayesian statistics assumes that we can combine probabilities obtained from data with probabilities that are the result of an *a priori* (prior) judgment.

We start by making a distinction between Bayesian methods in classical statistics and true Bayesian statistics. First, we look at Bayes' theorem and Bayesian methods in classical statistics. Consider two events A and B and all the associated probabilities, P, of their occurring:

$$P(A), P(B), P(A \cap B), P(A|B), P(B|A).$$

Using the rules of elementary probability, we can write

$$P(A|B) = \frac{P(A \cap B)}{P(B)}, P(B|A) = \frac{P(A \cap B)}{P(A)}$$

$$P(A|B)P(B) = P(B|A)P(A)$$

$$P(A|B) = \frac{P(B|A)P(A)}{P(B)}.$$

The last line of this equation is Bayes' theorem, a simple theorem of elementary probability theory. It is particularly useful because it helps solve *reverse* problems, such as the following: Suppose there are two bowls of cookies in a kitchen. One bowl contains 20 chocolate cookies, and the other bowl contains 10 chocolate cookies and 10 vanilla cookies. A child sneaks into the kitchen and, in a hurry so as not to be caught, chooses at random one cookie from one bowl. The cookie turns out to be a chocolate cookie. What is the probability that the cookie was taken from the bowl that contains only chocolate cookies? Bayes' theorem is used to reason about such problems.

We use the Bayesian scheme when we estimate the probability of *hidden* states or hidden variables. For example, in the cookie problem, we can observe the returns (the cookie taken by the child) and we want to determine in what market state the returns were generated (what bowl the cookie came from). A widely used Bayesian method to solve the problem is the Kalman filter.

A Kalman filter assumes that we know how returns are generated in each market state. The filter uses a Bayesian method to recover the sequence of states from observed returns. In these applications, Bayes' theorem is part of classical statistics and probability theory.

Now consider true Bayesian statistics. The conceptual jump made by Bayesian statistics is *to apply Bayes' theorem not only to events but to statistical hypotheses themselves*, with a meaning totally different from the meaning in classical statistics. Bayes' theorem in Bayesian statistics reads

$$P(H|A) = \frac{P(A|H)P(H)}{P(A)},$$

where H is not an event but a statistical hypothesis, $P(H)$ is the judgmental, prior probability assigned to the hypothesis, and $P(H|A)$ *is the updated probability after considering data A*. The probability after considering the data is obtained with the classical methods of statistics; the probability before considering the data is judgmental.

In this way, an asset manager's judgment can be commingled with statistics in the classical sense. For example, with Bayesian statistics, an asset manager can make model forecasts conditional on the level of confidence that he has in a given model. The manager can also average the forecasts made by different models, each with an associated prior probability that reflects his confidence in each single model.

Note that Bayesian priors might come not only from judgment but also from theory. For example, they can be used to average the parameters of different models without making any judgment on the relative strength of each model (uninformative priors).

Both classical and Bayesian statistics are ultimately rooted in data. Classical statistics uses data plus prior estimation principles, such as the maximum likelihood estimation principle; Bayesian statistics allows us to commingle probabilities derived from data with judgmental probabilities.

Another instance of exercising oversight is in the area of risk. One source said, "The only overlay we exercise is on risk, where we allow ourselves a small degree of freedom, not on the model."

One source summarized the key attributes of a quantitative process by defining the process as one in which a *mathematical* process identifies overvalued and undervalued stocks based on *rigorous* models; the process allows for *little portfolio manager discretion* and entails *tight tracking error and risk control*. The phenomena modeled, the type of models used, and the relative weights assigned may vary from manager to manager; different risk measures might be used; optimization might be fully automated or not; and a systematic fundamental overlay or oversight may be part of the system but be held to a minimum.

Does Overlay Add Value?

Because in practice many equity investment management processes allow a judgmental overlay, the question is: Does that fundamental overlay add value to the quantitative process?

We asked participants what they thought. As **Figure 2.1** depicts, two-thirds of survey participants disagreed with the statement that the most effective equity portfolio management process combines quantitative tools and a fundamental overlay. Interestingly, most of the investment consultants and fund-rating firms we interviewed shared the appraisal that adding a fundamental overlay to a quantitative investment process does not add value.

Figure 2.1. Response to: The Most Effective Equity Portfolio Management Process Combines Quantitative Tools and a Fundamental Overlay

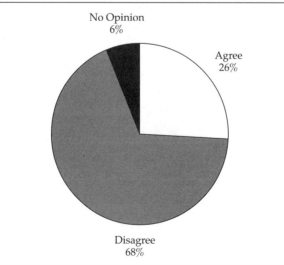

A source at a large consultancy said, "Once you believe that a model is stable—effective over a long time—it is preferable not to use human overlay because it introduces emotion, judgment. The better alternative to human intervention is to arrive at an understanding of how to improve model performance and implement changes to the model."

Some sources believe that a fundamental overlay has value in extreme situations, but not everyone agrees. One source said, "Overlay is additive and can be detrimental; oversight is neither. It does not alter the quantitative forecast but implements a reality check. In market situations such as of July–August 2007, overlay would have been disastrous. The market goes too fast and takes on a crisis aspect. It is a question of intervals."

Among the 26 percent who believe that a fundamental overlay does add value, sources cited the difficulty of putting all information in the models. A source that provides models for asset managers said, "In using quant models, there can be data issues. With a fundamental overlay, you get more information. It is difficult to convert all fundamental data, especially macro information such as the yen/dollar exchange rate, into quant models."

A source at a firm that is systematically using a fundamental overlay said, "The question is how you interpret quantitative outputs. We do a fundamental overlay, reading the 10-Qs and the 10-Ks and the footnotes plus looking at, for example, increases in daily sales, invoices.[13] I expect that we will continue to use a fundamental overlay; it provides a commonsense check. You cannot ignore real-world situations."

The same source noted, however, that the downside of a fundamental overlay can be its quality: "The industry as a whole is pretty mediocre, and I am not sure fundamental analysts can produce results. In addition, the fundamental analyst is a costly business monitor compared to a $15,000 computer."

These concerns raise the issue of measuring the value added by a fundamental overlay. Firms that we talked to that are adopting a hybrid quant/fundamental approach mentioned that they will be doing performance attribution to determine just who or what adds value. (This aspect is discussed further in the next section.)

An aspect that, according to some sources, argues in favor of using a fundamental overlay is the ability of an overlay to deal with concentration. A consultant to the industry said, "If one can get the right balance, perhaps the most effective solution is one where portfolio managers use quant tools and there is a fundamental overlay. The issue with the quant process is that a lot of investment managers struggle with estimating the risk-to-return ratio due to concentration. With a fundamental process, a manager can win a lot or lose a lot. With a pure quantitative

---

[13]The annual report in Form 10-K provides a comprehensive overview of a company's business and financial condition and includes audited financial statements. The quarterly report in Form 10-Q includes unaudited financial statements and provides a continuing view of the company's financial position during the year.

process, one can't win a lot: there is not enough idiosyncrasy. Hedge funds deal with the risk issue through diversification, using leverage to substitute for concentration. But this is not the best solution. It is here—with the risk issue, in deciding to increase bets—that the fundamental overlay is important."

There is no obvious rigorous way to handle overlays. Scientifically speaking, introducing human judgment into the models can be done by using Bayesian priors. Priors allow the asset manager or analyst to quantify unique events or, at any rate, events whose probability cannot be evaluated as relative frequency. The problem is how an asset manager gains knowledge of prior probabilities relative to rare events. Quantifying the probability of an event from intuition is a difficult task. Bayesian statistics gives rules for reasoning in a logically sound way about the uncertainty of unique events, but such analysis does not offer any hint about how to determine the probability numbers. Quantifying the probability of unique events in such a way as to ensure that the process consistently improves the performance of models is no easy task. (See the box titled "Can Uncertainty Be Measured?")

Can Uncertainty Be Measured?

We are typically uncertain about the likelihood of such events as future returns. Uncertainty can take three forms. First, uncertainty may be based on frequencies; this concept is used in classical statistics and in many applications of finance theory. Second, there is the concept of uncertainty in which we believe that we can subjectively assign a level of confidence to an event although we do not have the past data to support our view. The third form is *Knightian uncertainty*, in which we cannot quantify the odds for or against a hypothesis because we simply do not have any information that would help us resolve the question. (Frank H. Knight, 1885–1972, was a noted University of Chicago economist and was the first to make the distinction between *risk* and *uncertainty*. See Knight 1921.)

Classical statistics quantifies uncertainty by adopting a *frequentist* view of probability; that is, it equates probabilities with relative frequencies. For example, if we say there is a 1 percent probability that a given fund will experience a daily negative return in excess of 3 percent, we mean that, on average, every 100 days, we expect to see one day when negative returns exceed 3 percent. The qualification "on average" is essential because a probability statement leaves any outcome possible. We cannot jump from a probability statement to certainty. Even with a great deal of data, we can only move to probabilities that are closer and closer to 1 by selecting ever larger data samples.

If we have to make a decision under uncertainty, we must adopt some principle that is outside the theory of statistics. In practice, in the physical sciences, we assume that we are uncertain about individual events but are nearly certain when very large numbers are involved. We can adopt this principle because the numbers involved are truly enormous (for example, in 1 mole, or 12 grams, of carbon, there are approximately 600,000,000,000,000,000,000,000 atoms!).

In finance theory and practice, and in economics in general, no sample is sufficiently large to rule out the possibility that the observed (sample) distribution is different from the true (population) distribution—that is, to rule out the possibility that our sample is a rare sample produced by chance. In addition, many important events with a bearing on asset management are basically unique events. For example, a given corporate merger will either happen or it will not.

Nevertheless, the notion of uncertainty and the apparatus of probability theory are important in finance. Why? Because we need to make financial decisions and we need to compare forecasts that are uncertain so that we can eventually optimize our decisions.

This idea leads to the second notion of uncertainty, in which we evaluate the level of uncertainty at a judgmental level. For example, we believe that we can quantify the uncertainty surrounding the probability of a specific corporate merger. Clearly, a frequentist interpretation of uncertainty would not make sense in this case because we have no large sample from which to compute frequency. Theory does not tell us how to form these judgments, only how to make the judgments coherent. Bayesian theory (see the box titled "Bayesian Statistics") tells us how to commingle intuitive judgments with data.

As for Knightian uncertainty, Knight (1921) pointed out that in many cases, we simply do not know. Thus, we cannot evaluate any measure of likelihood. The situation of complete ignorance is subjective but very common: Given the information we have, there are countless questions for which we do not have any answer or any clue. For example, we might have no clue as regards the future development of a political crisis.

The bottom line is that the application of probability always involves a judgmental side. This aspect is obvious in judgmental and Knightian uncertainty, but it is true, if not so obvious, even in the classical concept of probability. In fact, even if we have sufficient data to estimate probabilities—which is rarely the case in finance—we always face uncertainty about whether the sample is truly representative. This uncertainty can be solved only at the level of judgment.

Bayesian priors are *a priori* judgments that will be modified inside the model by the data, but overlays might also be exercised at the end of the forecasting process. For example, overlays can be obtained by averaging a manager's forecasts with the model forecasts. This task also is not easy. In fact, it is difficult to make judgmental forecasts of a size sufficient to make them compatible with the model forecasts, which would make averaging meaningful.

Rise of the Hybrid Approach

Among the participants in the study, slightly more than half come from firms that use both fundamental and quantitative processes. The two businesses are typically run separately, but sources at these firms mentioned the advantage for quant managers of having access to fundamental analysts.

A source at a large firm known as a quantitative manager said, "It is important to have fundamental analysts inside an organization to bring fundamental insight. We don't use fundamental overrides in our quant funds, but if one wants to make a big move, a fundamental view can be of help—for example, if a model suggests to buy shares in a German bank when the fundamental analyst knows that German banks are heavily invested in subprime."

Although quantitative managers might turn to in-house fundamental analysts or their brokers before making major moves, perhaps the most interesting thing that is happening, according to several industry observers, is that fundamental managers are embracing quantitative processes. Indeed, in discussing quantitative equity management, a source at a large international investment consultancy remarked, "The most obvious phenomenon going on is that fundamental processes are introducing elements of quantitative analysis, such as quantitative screening." The objective in adding quant screens is to provide a decision-support tool that constrains the manager's choices.

A source in which fundamental managers are using quantitative-based screening systems said, "The quant-based screening system narrows the opportunity set and gives fundamental managers the tools of analysis. Our research center works with fundamental managers on demand, creating screening systems by using criteria that are different from those used by the quants."

Of the participating firms with fundamental processes backed up by stock-screening systems, one-third mentioned that it was an upward trend at their firms. One of the drivers behind the trend is the success of quantitative managers in introducing new products, such as 130–30 and similar strategies.[14]

A source that models for the buy side said, "Having seen the success of the 130–30 strategies, fundamental firms are trying to get into the quant space. Many of them are now trying to introduce quantitative processes, such as stock-screening systems."

Some quantitative managers (especially those at firms with large fundamental groups) believe that combining the discipline of quant screens with fundamental insight may be the trend in the future. A manager at a quant boutique that is part of a larger group that includes a large fundamental business said, "A lot of fundamental managers are now using stock-scoring systems. I expect that a fundamental-based element will be vindicated. The plus of fundamental managers is that they actually know the firms they invest in. With ranking systems, you get the quant discipline plus the manager's knowledge of a firm. Quants, on the other hand, have only a characteristic-based approach." For this source, combining the two approaches—judgmental and quantitative—solves the oft-cited problem of differentiation among quant products when everyone is using the same data and similar models. Indeed, the diminishing returns with quantitative processes and the need to find independent diversified sources of alpha were cited by some sources as motivations for their firms' interest in a hybrid quant/fundamental investment management process.

---

[14]A 130–30 fund is one that is constrained to be 130 percent long and 30 percent short so that the net (long minus short) exposure to the market is 100 percent. (Note that the "gross" exposure, long plus short positions, of such a fund is 160 percent.)

One source from a firm best known for its fundamental approach said, "I believe that fundamental managers get returns because they have information no one else has, versus quants, who do a better analysis to tease out mispricings. But the lode is being mined now with faster data feeds. I can see our firm going toward a hybrid style of management to have independent, diversified sources of alpha."

Sources that see their firms moving toward a hybrid process agree that a fundamental approach is likely to produce more alpha ("less-than-stellar" performance is an oft-cited drawback in marketing quantitative products) but bring more volatility. Reducing volatility is when the discipline of a quant process comes in. A head of quantitative equity said, "Maybe a fundamental manager with a 25-stock portfolio can produce more alpha, but we would see an increase in volatility. This is why I can see our firm doing some joint quant/fundamental funds with the fundamental manager making the call."

Firms that are introducing quantitative screens for their fundamental managers are also introducing other quantitative processes—typically, for performance attribution, accountability, and risk control. This move is not surprising because, although screens rate stocks, they do not provide the information needed to understand diversification and factor exposure. A source at a large traditional asset management firm that is introducing quantitative processes in its fundamental business said, "The firm has realized the value of quant input and will adopt quant processes for stock ranking as well as risk management, returns attribution, and portfolio composition."

Just as firms with fundamental processes are interested in quantitative processes as a diversified source of alpha, firms with quantitative processes are showing an interest in fundamental processes for the same reason. Some firms known as quant shops are taking a fresh look at fundamental processes, albeit disciplined with stock-ranking systems and risk control. A source at a large organization known for its systematic approach to asset management said, "Presently, only a small percentage of our business is run by fundamental managers. Going forward, we would like to grow this significantly. It is a great diversifier. But there will be accountability. Fundamental analysts will keep their own portfolios, but quantitative methods will be used for screening, performance attribution, accountability, and risk control."

Certainly, the good performance of quantitative managers in the value market of 2000–2005 attracted the attention of fundamental managers. And the more recent poor performance of quantitative funds, described in detail in Chapter 5, is causing some rethinking among quantitative managers. The need to find diversified sources of alpha to smooth over performance in growth *or* value market cycles is an important driver.

An industry observer commented, "What is successful in terms of producing returns—fundamental or quant—is highly contextual. A fusion of the two is likely, but it is difficult to say."

Some sources, however, questioned whether the recent poor performance of quantitative funds would have a negative impact on firms' intentions to implement hybrid quant/fundamental funds. The global head of quantitative strategies at a large firm said, "There are no walls between quant and fundamental. Quant funds had been doing very well the past four or five years, so management got interested and hybrid quant/fundamental funds were growing. But now, given the recent poor performance of quants, I expect to see this hybridization shrink."

Toward Full Automation?

Having a quantitative-driven process does not necessarily involve implementing a fully automated process. In such a process, investment decisions are made by computers with little or no human intervention. An automated process includes the input of data, production of forecasts, optimization/portfolio formation, oversight, and trading.

As noted at the outset of this chapter, most quantitative processes at sources allow at least a minimal level of oversight, and some allow a fundamental overlay. We asked participants whether they thought quantitative-driven equity investment processes were moving toward full automation.

Figure 2.2 shows that among those expressing an opinion, as many believe that quantitative managers are moving toward full automation as do not believe it. Apparently, we will continue to see a variety of management models. As mentioned

Figure 2.2. Response to: Most Quant-Driven Equity Investment Processes Are Moving toward Full Automation

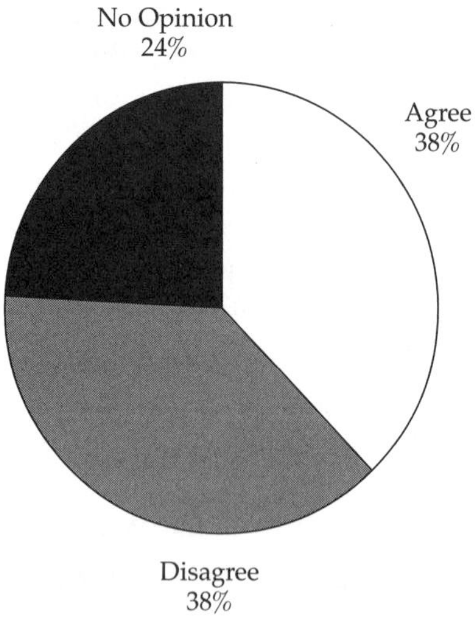

No Opinion
24%

Agree
38%

Disagree
38%

in Chapter 1, this diversity arises from the fact that there is no hard science behind quantitative equity investment management; business models reflect the personalities and skills inside an organization.

An industry observer remarked, "There are all degrees of automation among quants, and we see no obvious trend either toward or away from automation. Some quants use a small judgmental overlay; others are very quant, with an optimization model with risk tolerance profiles fed to the optimizer. Others use models plus judgment to avoid risk. Is one better than the other? It depends on the specifics: Is the model very robust? Does it produce what it should? The important thing is why people do what they do. If there is human interaction, why? What have you seen in the past that leads you to use a judgmental overlay? There are an incalculable number of ways of doing things. What works well for one will not work well for another."

We asked investment consultants how they and their clients felt about putting their investments with a fully automated fund. Responses were mixed. A source at an international investment consultancy said, "Our clients are not worried about fully automated processes." But another consultant said, "We are not keen on fully automated processes. We like to see human interaction, intervention before and after optimization, and especially before trading. The asset manager needs to know about corporate events, takeovers, and the like." Note, however, that this type of "human interaction" is more an instance of oversight than of a true overlay. Ultimately, models no doubt need at least some oversight because the models cannot factor in last-minute information that might have an impact on the price of an asset.

3. Business Issues

One objective of this study was to examine business issues, including motivations for implementing a quantitative process, barriers to entering the market, and issues related to marketing quantitatively managed funds.

Why Implement a Quantitative Process?

Figure 3.1 provides the full list that was given to survey participants of possible motives for adopting a "quant" equity investment process. In this type of question, survey participants were asked to rate the various items on a scale of 1 to 5; the bar chart provides the total rating each item received. According to Figure 3.1, three main objectives were behind the decision to adopt (at least partially) a quantitative process—tighter risk control, more stable returns, and better overall performance. The profile of a firm's founder(s) and/or the prevailing in-house culture were correlated with these objectives in that the profiles provided the requisite environment.

That quantitative processes might bring tighter risk control and better performance was corroborated in a study by Casey, Quirk & Associates (2005) titled "The Geeks Shall Inherit the Earth?" It tracked the performance of quantitative funds in the U.S. large-capitalization sector. The research universe included 32 quant managers managing 70 products with total assets of $157 billion and 387 "other" managers managing 688 products with total assets of $925 billion. The study found that for the 2002–04 period, quantitative-driven processes did indeed deliver better performance with tighter risk control. A source at Casey, Quirk & Associates said, "What we have seen is that quant managers clearly outperformed fundamental managers when you take into consideration the type of returns. In our study, which examined U.S. large-cap returns for the three-year period 2002–2004, the most compelling finding was that quant managers outperformed fundamental managers with half the risk. Quant managers as a group are better at quantifying the all-around risks and what is likely to go wrong."

Other major objectives behind the decision to implement a quantitative equity investment process include diversification in general or the desire to diversify into new products, such as 130–30 and similar strategies, and scalability, including the ability to scale to various "universes" or asset-class mandates. Regarding diversification of the asset manager's business, a source at a large asset management firm with a small quant group said, "An important motivating factor is diversification of the overall product lineup. Management believes that quant and fundamental products will not move in synch."

Figure 3.1. Factors behind a Firm's Motivation to Adopt (at Least Partially) a Quantitatively Driven Equity Investment Management Process as Rated by Survey Participants

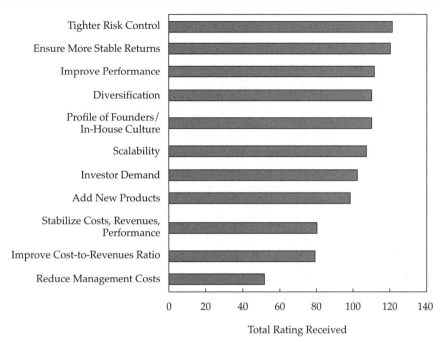

As for the ability to offer new products, a source at a sell-side firm modeling for the buy side remarked, "We are seeing a lot of interest by firms known for being fundamental that now want to introduce quant processes in the form of screens or other techniques. These firms are trying to get into the quant space, and it is the 130–30-type product that is pushing managers in this direction."

A general belief among those surveyed is that quantitatively managed funds outperform fundamental managers in the 130–30-type arena. The ability to backtest the strategy was cited as giving quantitatively managed funds the edge. A manager at a firm that offers both fundamental and quantitative products said, "Potential clients have told us that new products, such as the 130–30 strategies, are more believable with extensive quant processes and testing behind them."

In general, sources believe that quantitative processes give an edge whenever a complex problem needs to be solved. An investment consultant remarked, "Quant has an advantage when there is an element of financial engineering. The investment process is the same, but quant adds value when it comes to picking components and coming up with products such as 130–30."

Another source added, "A quant process brings the ability to create structured products. In the United States, institutional investors are using structured products especially in fixed income and hedge funds. Given the aging of the population, I would expect more demand in the future from private investors who want a product that will give them an income and act as an investment vehicle, such as a combination of an insurance-type payout and the ability to decompose and build up products."

As for scalability, a consultant to the industry remarked, "One benefit a quantitative process brings to management firms is the ability to apply a model quickly to a different set of stocks. For example, a firm that had been applying quant models to U.S. large cap was also able to test these models (in the back room) in 12–15 other major markets. Once they saw that the models had a successful in-house track record in different universes, they began to commercialize these funds."

Among survey participants, the desires to stabilize costs, revenues, and performance or to improve the cost-to-revenue ratio were rated relatively low as motivating factors for introducing quantitative processes. But one source at a large asset management firm said that stabilizing costs, revenues, and performance was an important factor in the firm's decision to embrace a quantitative process. According to this source, "Over the years, the firm has seen great consistency in a quant process: Fees, revenues, and costs are all more stable, more consistent than with a fundamental process."

Bringing management costs down was rated by participants as the weakest factor behind the drive to implement a quantitative equity investment process. A source at a large asset management firm with a small quantitative group said, "Has management done a cost–benefit analysis of quant versus fundamental equity investment management? Not to my knowledge. I was hired a few years ago to start up a quant process. But even if management had done a cost–benefit analysis and found quant attractive, it would not have been able to move into a quant process quickly. The average institutional investor has a seven-man team on the fund. If you were to switch to a two-man quant team, 80 percent of the clients would go away. Management has to be very careful; clients do not like to see change."

Another source at a large fundamental manager concurred, "Cost–benefit analysis was not a factor in the firm's decision to use quant. It was more a question of product offerings—for example, 130–30 and market-neutral strategies for institutional clients."

Although cost was not a major consideration in firms' decisions to adopt quantitative processes, we found some evidence that (large) firms with a quantitative process are more profitable than those run fundamentally. A consultant to the industry that ran a study of the issue said, "There is an aversion of fundamental asset managers to a quant process because they believe that it will lower the fees. If you look at the published fee schedules, it is definitely true that fees for a quant-run active equity fund are about 40–50 percent below those of a fundamentally managed fund. So, if you look at top-line revenues, there is less to play with if the process is quant. If one is a small player, it is probably better to be fundamental, but with a quant process, above a certain size, there are huge scale benefits. Our study included a research universe of some 40 firms managing more than $9 trillion. What we found was that quant firms were more profitable by far. The idea that quant firms are less profitable is false. Actually, if a firm is large enough, the quant process is vastly more profitable. This profitability comes from the fact that (1) a quant process can be scaled to different universes all run by the same team and (2) a quant process allows more strategies about when and how to trade."

Barriers to Entrance

The mid-2005 study by the consulting firm Casey, Quirk & Associates (2005) attributed 46 percent of market share in the U.S. large-cap active equity quantitative products arena to just three managers—Barclays Global Investors, LSV Asset Management, and Intech (a subsidiary of Janus Capital Group). Since that study, a few more firms have muscled their way to the top and the number of quant firms offering quant products has continued to grow. Firms such as Charles Schwab, Old Mutual, and the Vanguard Group have jumped into the active quant arena by proposing quantitative strategies, buying quant boutiques, and/or building up in-house teams.

When we asked survey participants what they thought about market concentration in the future, as **Figure 3.2** indicates, 77 percent of respondents said they believe that the active quantitative arena will continue to be characterized by the dominance of a few large players and a large number of small quant boutiques. Only 10 percent disagreed with this conclusion.

A consultant to the industry said, "Because quant has received so much attention, other managers are trying to introduce a quant approach. It is not a bad idea for fundamental shops, but for most, it is too little too late. Large quantitative firms have huge staffs of PhDs and are run like a university. There is already such a big concentration of assets and talents at large quant firms that introducing a quant approach is going to be harder because, from the point of view of the investor, it is not going to be credible. But giant groups don't have all the answers. If a brilliant professor comes up with a brilliant idea, he can make it. But standards are now much higher."

An investment consultant added, "It will be difficult for even the big newcomers to the active quant space who are introducing active quant as a different source of alpha."

We asked participants to rate a number of factors as barriers to new entrants into the quant equity investment space. As **Figure 3.3** reports, the most important barrier participants pointed out is the prevailing in-house culture. One source at a fundamental-oriented firm said that few firms are seriously opposed to trying to add discipline and improve performance by applying some quant techniques; the problem is that it is not so easy to change an organization.

Figure 3.2. Response to: Quantitative Equity Portfolio Management Will Continue to Be Characterized by the Domination of a Few Large Players and a Large Number of Small Quant Boutiques

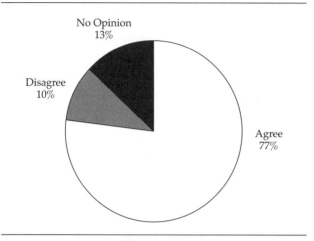

Figure 3.3. Barriers to New Entrants into the Quantitative Equity Investment Space as Rated by Survey Participants

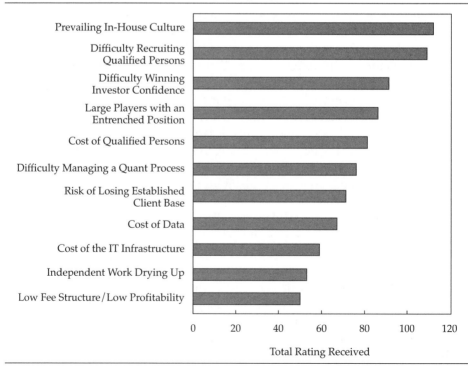

A source at a large international investment consultancy commented, "For a firm that is not quant endowed, it is difficult to make the shift from individual judgment to a quant process. Those that have been most successful in terms of size in the active quant arena are those that began in passive quant [that is, indexing]. They chose passive because they understood it would be easier for a quantitative process to perform well in passive as opposed to active management. Most of these firms have been successful in their move to active quant management."

A source at a large firm with fundamental and quant management styles said, "Can a firm with a fundamental culture go quant? It is doable, but the odds of success are slim. Fundamental managers have a different outlook, and these are difficult times for quants."

Difficulty in recruiting qualified people was rated the second most important barrier. "Recruiting the right skills," one source said, "is a major obstacle." The cost of qualified people was considered a less important barrier.

Next came difficulty in gaining investor confidence, followed by the entrenched position of market leaders. An industry observer remarked, "What matters most is the investment culture and market credibility. If an investor does not believe that the manager has quant as a core skill, the manager will not be credible in the arena of quant products. There is the risk that the effort will be perceived by the investor as a back-room effort with three people, understaffed and undercommitted."

An investment consultant added, "We look at the number of people involved and their credibility. Whether the process is fundamental or quant, there is always an element of risk if it is a question of only one or a few people. If the team is small, it leads to questions such as: What happens if the senior person goes? Or, in the case of a quant fund: What if the person who designed the models goes? With a large firm, if a key person leaves, it is not a problem."

Gaining investor confidence is, of course, key to getting the assets to manage. A source at a firm with both fundamental and quantitative strategies said, "You will need to demonstrate that you know what you are doing in the quant space before clients will be comfortable." Another source at a firm with both fundamental and quant strategies underlined the chicken-or-egg dilemma in gaining investors' confidence and investors' assets. According to the source, "If the principal business is long only, you need to manage a lot of assets. A start-up needs long-term assets to fund the business, and it is hard to get these assets. Scale is an important barrier."

The fear of losing existing clients was rated relatively low, perhaps because one-third of the participants are 100 percent quant. But some sources from firms with both fundamental and quant processes rated fear of losing existing clients as a very high barrier to the introduction of quant processes. A source from a firm with a large fundamental organization said, "If the firm were to shift from a fundamental process to a quant process, it would be a red flag to our clients."

The cost of data and of the information technology (IT) infrastructure were considered by participants to have relatively little importance as a barrier to entry. Computer costs continue to fall, and although data can be expensive, data suppliers use pricing discretion. A source that models for the buy side commented, "The cost of data is not an obstacle. Data suppliers price lower for smaller firms. It is a question of growing the client base."

Nor did participants attribute much importance as a barrier to entry to a drying up of academic research or to the low fee structure/low profitability of a quant process. The low fee structure typically associated with a quant process is more typical of passive quant. A source at a large international investment consultancy said, "Active quant fees are not significantly lower than fundamental active fees. If a fundamental active fee is 60 bps on large cap, active quant is 45–50 bps." Indeed, 90 percent of the survey respondents disagreed with the statement that a quantitative approach to asset management generates low fees and so is less profitable to the asset management firm.

To summarize, asset managers and industry observers believe that the quant arena will continue to be characterized by a few large players plus a relatively large number of small quantitative boutiques. The most important barriers to entry are related to a firm's culture and the ability to recruit the right skills. If assets of the client base are being managed fundamentally, a firm's existing client base can also make change difficult. In the absence of a persistent clear-cut performance advantage for quantitative management, it is understandable that a firm's culture and existing client base constitute a major barrier to "going quant," although, as we have seen, they are not stopping the introduction of quantitative processes to add discipline and improve performance.

In many fields, given the cost, difficulty, and riskiness of trying to build up an engineering team capable of challenging market leaders, the depth of technical knowledge and the complexity of the engineering and production processes are barriers to entry. For example, only a handful of companies worldwide have the technical expertise to design and build jet engines. Starting a new venture to manufacture jet engines would require a tremendous amount of capital, commitment, and courage.

In the case of financial models, however, building a model is a technical accomplishment within the reach of a team formed by a handful of people, perhaps two or three academics plus an IT person and someone to "scrub" the data. If someone comes with modeling experience and has a bright idea and the nerves to test it with real money, then the barriers to entry are not insurmountable from a technical point of view.

Managing a group of modelers who must serve the needs of a diversified investment community, however, is a test of a different nature. And given that the main challenge of financial modeling is in managing a fundamentally uncertain process, models must be continuously updated and model results must be supervised. In the physical sciences, one encounters difficult problems and solutions require creative thinking, but once the problem is solved—barring mistakes—no uncertainty remains. In financial modeling, there is no real "solution," only local approximations. A model may be created and backtested, but in finance, no backtesting procedure is conclusive for two reasons. First, backtesting is typically performed on the same dataset as that used to come up with the ideas for the models. One can try to separate a test set from a learning set, but ultimately, as Paul Samuelson (1994) said, there is only one "run" of the past and that is all that we can study. Second, data are scarce, and even if we can backtest our models on 15 or 25 years of data, we have no guarantee that the model will perform on tomorrow's data. As any financial modeler knows, success can be elusive.

To illustrate the gap between finance and the hard sciences, recall that every asset manager's prospectus carries a warning similar to the following: "Investors should be aware that past performance is no guarantee of future performance." Imagine boarding an airplane with the following warning written on the ticket: "Passengers should be aware that the safety of past trips is no guarantee of the safety of this trip."

Marketing Quantitative Products

In a 2006 survey of trends in equity portfolio modeling (Fabozzi, Focardi, and Jonas 2007), participants remarked on difficulties encountered in marketing quantitative products. Some sources cited the fact that quantitative funds are based on a more complex process than fundamental funds and so are harder to explain and more difficult to sell to investors. Others noted that differentiating one quantitative product from another is hard. We asked participants in this study to rate the strength of various selling points of quantitative products.

Participants rated the most salient selling points in marketing quantitative products as shown in **Figure 3.4**. Not much difference separates the top five: alpha generation, enhanced investment discipline, risk management, transparency of the quantitative process, and diversification. Investment consultants agreed. One said, "The best way to sell a quant process is to make sure that it is presented as an alpha-capturing opportunity grounded in the real world and in academia (finance theory), not as clever math."

Technical arguments—such as the idea that a quantitative product is the result of a rule-based process, that quantitative processes eliminate style drift, or that such processes are nondiscretionary—followed the top five. Again, investment consultants' views were similar. The ability to reduce subjectivity was widely cited by consultants as a major advantage of a quantitatively driven process.

Figure 3.4. Relative Strength of Selling Points of a Quantitative Product as Rated by Survey Participants

One consultant commented, "There is a clear advantage of a quant approach over a fundamental approach: The quant approach is less susceptible to behavioral biases, and these biases are increasingly recognized as important to results. Quant processes are, of course, susceptible to biases because quant models are programmed by humans. If a modeler examines propositions that have worked well in the past and sets them up in the future, it might turn out that they worked in the past purely by chance. But quant processes are more systematic; they use more math skills."

Another consultant added, "A quant approach takes out the weaknesses of humans, the behavioral biases. It is objective and has a standard, repeatable way of looking at things. One stock is looked at in the same way as another. The quant process strips out the subjectivity. This is a main selling point of a quant process. The successful active fundamental manager is almost like a machine: He does not fall in love with a stock or a CFO [chief financial officer]—and he admits mistakes."

Lower management fees and lower trading costs were rated as less salient selling points. This rating for lower management fees should not be surprising because investment consultants noted that management fees for an active quantitative fund were perhaps only slightly lower than those for a traditionally run active fund.

Fees were an important consideration, however, for a source at a firm that evaluates fund performance on a risk-adjusted and fee-adjusted basis. This source cautioned, "We have noticed that the better performing funds are the low-cost ones. Active quant is attractive only if it can keep the management fees low. High fees and high risk taking are expensive hurdles."

As for lower trading costs, some investment consultants we talked to for the study gave execution issues a high rating, and on this matter, the advantage went to quantitative investment processes. A consultant said, "Quants are ahead in terms of transaction cost analysis and market impact. This is a huge advantage."

Transaction cost analysis has become a quantitative discipline in itself. Transaction costs have a fixed component (commissions and fees) plus a variable component (market impact cost, opportunity cost, and price-movement risk). In today's environment of electronic trading, market impact is by far the largest cost. The impact can be minimized by spreading the trade over two or more days. This choice introduces another risk, however, because prices may move in the interval. Transaction cost analysis evaluates this trade-off and produces an optimal trading strategy. Quantitative firms evaluate the opportunity of a trade versus the projected minimal cost of the transaction and make the trade only if profit exceeds costs. Transaction costs represent a serious limitation to the use of high-frequency data and to exploiting market inefficiencies at high frequency. For example, short-term reversals are a theoretical source of profit, but the transaction costs associated with strategies that trade daily wipe out that profit.

Interestingly, the fact that stock selection is (typically) based on statistical analysis was considered the weakest selling point by survey participants! An investment consultant commented, "It is considerably more difficult to sell a quant product than a traditionally managed one. Selling quant funds to clients makes an appeal to a different part of the brain. Most clients are not equipped to deal with statistical data—which is why the argument being used to market quant funds is their track record. Because a lot of quant processes have been pretty successful, they can use this as a sales argument."

We also asked sources what they consider the major factors holding back investments in active quantitative products. As **Figure 3.5** shows, sources identified lack of acceptance/understanding on the part of investors as the major blocking factor. Investment consultants serving institutional clients commented, however, that investor appetite is there if the performance is there.

Figure 3.5. Factors Holding Back Investments in Active Quantitative Equity Products as Rated by Survey Participants

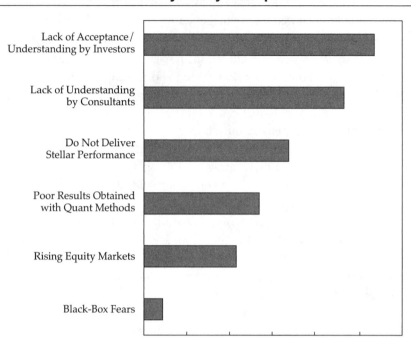

A source at a large international investment management consultancy said, "It is not necessarily difficult to sell quant strategies to an institutional investor. There are various types of investors. Some 20 percent would never invest in a quant fund by nature, and it would be impossible to sell a quant product to them. But with clients that are willing to listen and take the time to understand, it is not hard (it is not easy either) to sell a quant product."

Another investment consultant added, "There is now a greater understanding among investors about quant processes and what they can deliver, the value added. Investors have understood that the quant process is a highly systematic, organized, statistical formulation of the investment challenge."

Nevertheless, survey participants rated the lack of understanding of quant processes by consultants themselves as the second most important obstacle holding back investments in active quant products. As one quantitative manager at an essentially fundamental firm noted, "Quant products are unglamorous. There are no 'story' stocks, so it makes it a hard sell for consultants to their clients."

The need to educate consultants and investors alike to gain their confidence was cited by several sources as a major challenge for the future. **Figure 3.6** contains a question in the survey about the need for disclosure in light of the poor performance of quant funds since July–August 2007. As Figure 3.6 shows, educating investors might require more disclosure about quant processes—at least according to slightly fewer than half of the survey participants.

Figure 3.6. Response to: In View of Recent Poor Performance of Some Quantitative Equity Funds, Quantitative Managers Will Be under Pressure by Investors to Disclose More about Their Processes

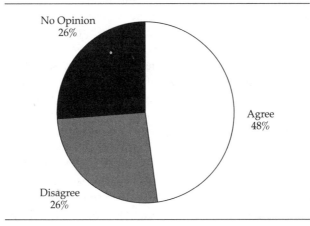

One chief investment officer (CIO) of equities who believes that greater disclosure will be required remarked, "Following events of summer 2007, quants will need to be better in explaining what they do and why it ought to work. They will need to come up with a rationale for what they are doing. They will have to provide more 'proof-of-concept' statements."

The CIO of equities at another firm disagreed: "One lesson from the events of July–August 2007 is that we will be more circumspect when describing what we are doing. Disclosing what one is doing can lead to others replicating the process and thus a reduction of profit opportunities."

Lack of outstanding ("stellar") performance, as Figure 3.5 shows, was rated a moderately important factor in holding back investments in quantitative funds. Less-than-stellar performance can be balanced by a greater consistency in performance. A source at a fund-rating service said, "Because quant funds are broadly diversified, returns are watered down. Quants do not hit the ball out of the park, but they deliver stable performance."

The ability to deliver stable, if not stellar, performance can, of course, be turned into a major selling point. Quantitative managers cite how General Manager Billy Beane of the Oakland Athletics improved his team's performance by using cybermetrics, the analysis of baseball through objective (i.e., statistical) evidence. This analysis led Beane to shift his emphasis from acquiring players who hit the most home runs or who seemed most talented when evaluated by scouts to acquiring players with the most consistent records of getting on base.[15] Beane also recruited players who were inexpensive because their talents were not obvious to other teams that did not use statistical analysis. As a result, Beane is credited with having made the Oakland Athletics the most cost-effective team in baseball, although winning the American League Championship Series has proven elusive for them.

Figure 3.5 shows that poor results and rising equity markets were rated low as factors holding back investment in active quant funds. Quantitative products went through a period of good performance in the value market of 2001–2005, which, according to sources, saw inflows into active quantitative funds outpace those into traditionally managed active equity funds. Speaking just before the events of July–August 2007, a source at a large investment consultancy said, "Given that active quant managers have been pretty successful in the past value market, flows into active quant have grown considerably in the past 12–36 months."

As mentioned previously, one problem that quantitative managers face in marketing their products is differentiation. Some sources view differentiation as the major challenge for the future. Fundamental managers have their stock stories to differentiate them, but quantitative managers work with data feeds and models. When everyone is using the same datasets and similar models, differentiation is challenging to achieve and to explain. The observation made by many participants that it is difficult to differentiate quant products means that it is difficult to find risk–return characteristics that are recognizably different from those of the competition.

Long-only funds differentiate by offering different exposures to different market sectors and indices. In addition, they are differentially exposed to factors other than sectors or indices. For example, they might be exposed to momentum factors. Market-neutral funds are typically sold as vehicles capable of offering positive returns (alpha) without exposure to market factors (beta). To say that these funds do not have market exposure is slightly misleading, however, because market-neutral funds are actually exposed to other factors. For example, the events of July–August 2007 made it clear that these funds are exposed to various common factors that experience reversion to the mean.

Differentiation of financial products is essentially a question of how these products will perform in the market when performance includes risk. To sell a fund on this basis requires (1) that the investment process and the underlying assumptions be disclosed and (2) that the investor have the ability to understand how a quantitative product will behave.

---

[15] As reported in Lewis (2003).

4. Implementing a Quant Process

Quantitative processes differ from firm to firm; so does implementation. As one source said, "There is no simple formula. Everything is unique." But whether the firm began as a "quant" firm, built the business inside, or built the quant side together with a traditionally managed business, the firm needs to marshal the requisite skills and technology. These include the ability to quantify information, build and backtest models, construct portfolios, run performance checks, and update models when required.

We asked investment consultants what they thought was most important in evaluating a quantitative investment process: the economic reasoning, the process, or the model. One source said, "Of the three, the most important is the process. But to understand the process, you need to know the philosophy and understand how it performs in specific markets—for example, in markets that are trending up, down, or sideways. You need to understand what drives the returns."

Another source said, "We are interested to see if the modeling approach is grounded in proper economic rationale, how the quant approach extracts value from finance theory. We are agnostic as to the model itself. We have seen many processes that are very simple but work and others that are complex and don't work. We look for robustness in terms of the construction."

Yet another consultant said, "We evaluate the process, the finance theory behind the models, and the models themselves. We look very closely at the latter and, in particular, at the statistical inference techniques."

Many asset managers, not quantitative hedge fund managers alone, reveal little to nothing to the outside world, however, about the assumptions underlying their processes and how their models work. These funds are, as one consultant remarked, "difficult to understand." The events of July–August 2007 revealed that many aggressively marketed quant funds that had been offering high returns were doing so not as a result of a superior investment process but because of leverage.

We will now take a look at how the industry manages the model-building process.

Quantifying Things

As one source said, "A quantitative process is a process that quantifies things." The notion of "quantifying things" is central to any modern science, including, in Thomas Carlyle's words, the "dismal science" of economics. Everything related to accounting at the company level, balance sheet and income statement data, and even accounting at the national level is, by nature, quantitative. So, in a narrow sense, finance has always been quantitative. The novelty is that we are now quantifying things that are not directly observable, such as risk, or things that are not quantitative per se, such as market sentiment.

Let us expand a moment on the notions of "quantity" and "measurement." Although quantitative sciences are empirical sciences, what is quantified is not necessarily directly observed. A key aspect of modern science is the use of quantities not directly observed but defined as theoretical terms. These terms are essential in the formulation of the theory. Obvious examples in the physical sciences are quantities such as temperature. One does not observe temperature directly: Temperature is a theoretical term quantified through other measurements and through a theory. In finance, a representative example is the measurement of risk. Risk is not observed but inferred by numbers such as value at risk (VaR) or volatility as calculated by a model.

Quantifying, therefore, is more than a question of establishing a process of measurement: It is the definition of a theoretical term that can be put into relationship with other observations. We are interested in quantifying things not because we want to attach a precise number to an event but because we believe that the new quantities will allow us to predict other observations.[16]

Modelers in finance quantify many qualitative and vaguely defined concepts because they believe the new quantities will help in making forecasts. For example, modelers believe quantifying market sentiment will be useful in creating factors that will help in forecasting returns. Another example is recognizing market states; here, quantification is replaced by categorization. The point is that such nonquantitative concepts can be integrated in a factor model: Quantifying and modeling are intertwined. (For a discussion of factor models, see the appendix, "Factor Models.")

Note that we do not quantify to make vague things precise.[17] Vague concepts remain vague; quantifying replaces nonquantitative concepts with precise quantitative ones. Typically, when we introduce a quantitative concept, we have an intuition but the quantity is not the precise measurement of our intuition. For example, when scientists began to create thermodynamics in the 18th century, the starting point was the observation that some things are warm and other things are

---

[16] Here, we are making a distinction between quantities that can be observed and quantities that can only be inferred on the basis of a combination of theory and measurements. Actually, a critical theme in the modern philosophy of science is that no quantity can actually be observed because the only pure observation is pure perception. Thus, we identify a hierarchy of quantities that can be observed within a certain level of science. We start with commonsense observations, accept a first level of measurement based on reading simple instruments, and progressively construct higher levels of science. At the top are all the theoretical constructs of, say, quantum mechanics.

[17] The desire to make vague concepts precise is deeply rooted in human psychology because it reduces uncertainty. A sick child might ask, "Mom, do I feel nauseous?" Of course, Mom does not know how the child feels; she can measure for a fever but not for nausea.

cold. The introduction of the concept of temperature does not, however, make our sensations more precise. Knowing that the temperature of the water is 14°C (57°F) does not help a swimmer determine whether she is comfortable or cold once in the water (although if the swimmer had known the temperature beforehand, she might not be in the water). By the same token, in quantifying market sentiment, we do not get a precise measurement of the "intensity of belief" of market analysts; we simply construct a quantity that is useful in forecasting.

No "exact" or "correct" quantification process exists. In line with modern science, the key requirement is that the quantification be useful in predicting an event. Consider the notion of risk. Risk is often said to be a "multifaceted" phenomenon, by which we mean that risk cannot be boiled down to a single measure but requires various measures to capture its various aspects. What happens is the following: We have an intuitive notion of risk and try to capture this notion with a measurement process, such as VaR. But then, we discover that many different quantities allow us to make different predictions about risk and that all of them are useful. So, we adopt a vector of risk measures that includes, for example, conditional VaR, beta, or even a distribution. These measures are not a faithful description of our vague intuition of risk; they are simply useful measurements of aspects of risk.

If financial modeling does not prescribe a correct way to quantify things, what are the possibilities? Many models use *hidden* quantities—that is, quantities that cannot be directly observed but that are inferred by the model. This type of modeling is an explicit procedure well known in financial econometrics. For example, in autoregressive conditional heteroscedastic (ARCH) and generalized autoregressive conditional heteroscedastic (GARCH) models or in stochastic volatility models, volatility is a hidden term. Sometimes, hidden terms can be approximately translated into direct observations. For example, hidden factors can typically be mimicked by portfolios. Estimating quantities that are hidden but well defined mathematically (for example, market states) is a major econometric problem. Its solution includes such breakthroughs as the expectation maximization (EM) algorithm (see Dellaert 2002; Dempster, Laird, and Rubin 1977).

We can also quantify things by creating categories. For example, models working on balance sheet data often need to categorize companies. Rather than use standard industry classifications, some firms use their own models (for example, clustering algorithms) to categorize companies. One participant said, "We use various techniques, including clustering, to group balance sheet data." Categorization thus obtained is a kind of hidden variable because it is not observed but *inferred* through a mathematical process.

In some cases, however, models need to quantify things that we do not know how to identify through a mathematical process. Market sentiment is one such thing. One way to quantify market sentiment is to use analysts' forecasts. For example, the modeler makes a quantitative evaluation of market sentiment simply by counting the percentage of analysts who issue buy versus sell versus hold recommendations for specific companies. This use of information is one way of converting judgmental data (e.g., analysts' forecasts) into numerical values. Sometimes, judgmental inputs are subject to a quality check before being incorporated in a model. The head of quantitative management at one firm said, "We take uncorrelated signals from 50 fundamental analysts and test how good a signal is from each analyst."

The discipline (and practice) of behavioral finance is based on the ability to construct working theories and/or models from data that express human behavior and its associated biases. In behavioral finance, one needs to measure the psychological state that leads to cognitive biases, such as overconfidence and belief persistence. In practice, measuring the overconfidence bias, for example, might translate into simply adopting a momentum model or it might lead to a detailed analysis of data and companies. An asset manager might study what combinations of balance sheet items and corporate behavior typically lead to analyst biases. The modeler might discover that an aggressive public relations campaign masks shortcomings in the balance sheet. The automated analysis of news, such as is presently offered by Reuters and Thomson Financial, can help in establishing behavioral strategies.

A source that is using behavioral biases in a bottom-up modeling process said, "We do our own conceptual thinking on behavioral finance and come up with our own way of reasoning on this. Our objective is to do more unique conceptual work, build more unique factors, by gathering data ourselves as well as using third-party data."

Clearly, the ability to quantify and the methodologies used to quantify play key roles in building a quantitative methodology. But what types of things that can be quantified and modeled will give an analytical edge?

Based largely on academic research, technical models use well-established methods to quantify hidden variables. In the fundamental models that are behind the widely used bottom-up approach to quantitative equity management, however, the challenge is to invent quantities that can be integrated into a global methodology. Credit Suisse (2007), for example, conducted extensive backtesting of more than 400 stock selection factors to create its aggregate five-factor groups: (1) valuation, (2) use of capital, (3) profitability, (4) growth, and (5) price momentum.

A critical question is: Do specific datasets provide a competitive advantage? We can turn the question around and ask: What types of things can I quantify and model that would give me an analytical edge?

Participants commented that quant managers now need much more detailed information than in the past to acquire an analytical edge, but this information is difficult to capture and use in modeling. A head of active quantitative equity research said, "To have an information edge, you need to go through accounting information or have insider information. We have noticed that one now needs far more detail to produce better returns—for example, looking at footnotes in the balance sheet, finding discrepancies in statements, understanding if there is a merger or acquisition in the works. The problem for quants is: How do you capture that information?"

We will return to this aspect in the discussion of strategies to improve performance in Chapter 5.

The Modeling Process

Financial models solve problems. Modelers are engaged in a continuous process of short-lived discoveries. That is, they will discover some regularity and implement a model based on it, but they know the model will soon need to be updated.

Numerical and Nonnumerical Models. Quantities are represented by numbers, and as one source said, "A quantitative process is a process that uses numerical information systematically." The numerical information is used to build models whose objective is to capture market inefficiencies. For example, a factor model of returns is based on numerical (hence, quantitative) relationships between factors and subsequent returns. But as noted in the introduction to this chapter, not all computer-assisted investment management procedures are quantitative. Various types of *nonnumerical algorithms* are being used in financial modeling. Rule-based systems are nonnumerical algorithms that make decisions based on a set of rules. The rules might be provided by human operators, in which case, we refer to the system as an "expert system." But rules might also be automatically "discovered"— for example, by decision trees.[18]

As **Figure 4.1** reports, among survey participants, numerical methods are by far the most widely used modeling methods. They are being used at 90 percent of the participating firms. Rule-based nonnumerical methods are being used at a quarter of the firms but are used as the exclusive modeling tool at only two. We believe these portions are representative of the industry as a whole. In the future, participants do not expect a significant change in their methods; rather, they expect reinforcement of their present modeling approaches.

Factor Models and Predictors. The most widely used numerical models are factor models. Factor models estimate risk or forecast returns as a function of the value of a number of factors. They serve two purposes. As risk models, they compute exposures to various factors and help compute the return covariance matrix

---

[18]A decision tree is an algorithm that discovers rules by partitioning sample data sequentially as a function of a sequence of questions. For example (this example is obviously not realistic), a decision tree might try to find a rule that links returns and trading volumes. The algorithm will begin by dividing sample data into quantiles—say, high, medium, and low. The algorithm will then partition sample data as if responding to a series of questions such as: Were trading volumes high, low, medium in the previous period? Were returns high, low, medium in the last three periods? And so on. At the end of the process, the decision tree will produce rules such as: If returns are high for three consecutive periods and trading volumes are low for three consecutive periods, then returns will be low in the next period.

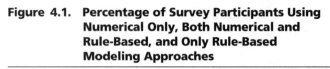

Figure 4.1. Percentage of Survey Participants Using Numerical Only, Both Numerical and Rule-Based, and Only Rule-Based Modeling Approaches

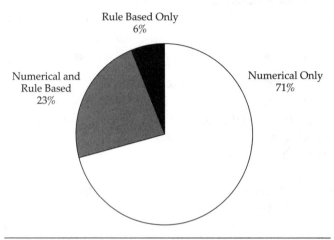

by reducing its dimensionality.[19] As forecasting models, they help form forecasts that depend on common determinants of asset returns.

When applied to portfolio returns as risk models, factor models compute the alphas and betas of the fund strategy. Generally in a multifactor model of a large economy, alphas, if they exist, are considered to be a sign of market inefficiency and thus a source of profit.[20] In a *forecasting factor model*, however, alphas can be all zero and the model might nevertheless reveal market inefficiencies and be a source of profit. Whether the Fama and French (1993) factor model reveals inefficiencies or not is still being debated.

Determining factors is not a trivial task. Statistical factor analysis and principal components analysis use the time series of returns to determine factors and estimate factor models. Factors thus determined are hidden, abstract factors. They are typically risk factors unless they are used in a "dynamic factor model" context (see the appendix, "Factor Models," for a description.)

Factors can also be determined by economic theory. The academic literature has identified a number of variables with explanatory or predictive power. Observable macroeconomic variables, such as interest rates or gross domestic product, can

---

[19]For example, the correlation matrix for 500 stocks has (500 × 499 ÷ 2 = 124,750) elements that need to be estimated. If each stock can be modeled as a vector of 10 factors, each multiplied by 10 factor exposures or loadings, the modeler needs to estimate only (10 × 9 ÷ 2 = 45) correlations plus the 10 factor loadings, for a total of 55 estimates. Only the second estimation problem can realistically be solved.

[20]Theory allows a (small) finite number of alphas to be nonzero (see the appendix, "Factor Models").

be used directly as factors; factor models are estimated as multiple regressions. Characteristics such as the price-to-earnings ratio are company-specific variables, however, and cannot be used directly as factors. Characteristics-based factors reconstruct factors constraining the model (see the appendix). They typically require that factor loadings be functions of the characteristics. Common factors are those that influence the returns of all or most of the stocks in the entire market.

A *predictive factor model* ignores variables that are idiosyncratic predictors of the returns of a specific stock. Mimicking the activity of a human manager, configurations of predictors can be used directly for predicting returns without the need to construct a factor model with common factors. For example, the returns of a stock might be predicted by the financial ratios of that specific company. Actually, there is no compelling theoretical reason to believe that a predictor should be common to the entire market. The relationship of returns to idiosyncratic predictors might be common to many stocks and many times. For example, some configuration of financial ratios might be a good predictor regardless of specific times and stocks.

Therefore, one might use cross-sectional data to look for nonlinear relationships between factors and returns or use clustering algorithms to find clusters of balance sheet data with predictive power. Note that, in general, nonlinear models require a great deal of data and thus are difficult to estimate. The use of cross-sectional data might offer a solution, but to look for the right pattern in large quantities of cross-sectional data requires strong economic intuition. A participant who is using cross-sectional data commented that cross-sectional data ease the problem of estimation but require attention in selecting the appropriate nonlinearities.

The market events of July–August 2007 made it evident that many firms were using the same factors or predictors. This state of affairs is hardly surprising in light of the fact that factor models are one of the most intensively researched subjects in financial modeling and their use is widespread. Because linear factors are relatively easily determined, the same factors will tend to be used by a large number of managers, which eliminates the profit from using them. Thus, unexploited profit opportunities are most likely to be found in the nonlinearities of the market.

Data Mining. In the 1990s, data mining was widely used to reveal predictive relationships in return time series. Data mining involves a set of machine learning methods used by statisticians and computer scientists to find rules and patterns in data *automatically* without human intervention and without the support of any theory. Experience has shown that a pure data-mining approach—at least at the level of mining time series of equity returns—is not feasible (see the box titled "Data Mining"). A leading investment consultant said, "I do not feel comfortable with a purely data-mining process. There is no economic reason why spurious relationships should exist. Beta loadings must be stable over a long period of time."

Data Mining

A few highly successful hedge funds are believed to use pure data-mining methodologies to find mispricings. As noted in the chapter text, data mining is a set of machine-learning methods used by statisticians and computer scientists to find rules and patterns in data *automatically*— without human intervention and without the support of any theory.

Data mining made its entrance into finance in the 1990s with the advent of high-performance workstations and low-cost supercomputers. Many asset managers and investment consultants who participated in the study reported here are skeptical, however, of the ability of pure data mining to find anything other than spurious relationships in applications of interest to investment management.

Initially, data mining was associated with artificial intelligence and the nascent fields of adaptive systems (with methodologies such as genetic algorithms) and self-organizing systems (with methodologies such as self-organizing maps). Two decades of experience have allowed us to gain a better understanding of the scope and methods of data mining.

Universal models (i.e., models that are able to capture any possible relationship) are key to data mining. One of the best known examples of a universal model is the neural network. A *neural network* is an adaptive mathematical model that learns from examples. It performs a series of iterations, adjusting its own parameters to better fit the given examples. If we allow a neural network to have any number of nodes and layers, it can approximate any curve with arbitrary precision. A typical application in finance is to use a neural network to learn the relationship between returns in different moments so that future returns can be predicted by past returns.

Clustering algorithms are another example of universal models, insofar as they can implement any partitioning of data up to the single unit. Clustering algorithms do not use examples but look at data and form partitions (or clusters) that are judged as a function of some cost criteria. Iteratively, clustering algorithms refine the partitions.

Given a sample of data, the many varieties of neural networks and clustering algorithms can effectively discover any pattern that exists in the sample data. Fine patterns are not necessarily true features, however, of the universe from which the sample data were extracted; they might be the result of unpredictable random noise. A crucial aspect of a data-mining algorithm, therefore, is to separate information from noise. The general methodology for performing this separation is to constrain the complexity of the data-mining algorithm so that it captures the important features, not the noise. The concepts of *information theory* may be used to assess the amount of information that can be extracted from a sample given its size.

Unfortunately, methodologies to separate signals from noise work well only if there is not much noise and if the sample is very large. In most financial applications, neither condition holds. Relative to the needs of learning algorithms, samples are small and the amount of noise is enormous. To understand the data problem, which is known as the "curse of dimensionality," consider learning an empirical multivariate distribution. Suppose we have 10 dimensions (e.g., 10 stock returns) and we "coarse-grain" each dimension in 10 intervals (i.e., we consider only 10 return intervals). There are a total of $10^{10} = 10,000,000,000$ multidimensional bins in which we have to place some data to estimate probabilities through relative frequencies. Unless we have billions of data points, this is an impossible task.

For these reasons, a pure data-mining approach is basically impossible. Applications of data mining to finance need the support of theory to guide the search. The only possible exception would be the derivatives markets. The reason is that in these markets, valuations are performed by computers. As demonstrated by Hutchinson, Lo, and Poggio (2004), it is technically feasible for a computer to learn the pricing algorithm of another computer. Learning different algorithms, the computer might find mispricings between derivative valuations and thereby make a good profit.

One area in which data mining might be profitably used is in derivatives trading because of the size of the market. The Bank for International Settlements estimated the value of over-the-counter derivatives to be $415 trillion at the end of 2006. This number is a large multiple of the total amount of stocks and bonds outstanding in the world. With such volume, small systematic regularities might exist in the patterns of prices and returns of derivatives portfolios. These regularities might be the result of differences or equivalences in the contracts that embody derivatives and in the valuation methodologies, not in the underlying economic processes. Given the enormous amount of data available, a data-mining algorithm might, for example, mimic how banks value and price derivatives. A number of high-profile hedge funds reportedly use such techniques.

Part of the appeal of data mining comes from the need to adapt to the continuously evolving markets. A consultant to the industry remarked, "Linear methods are easier to implement, conceptually simpler, and require less computing power, but the industry is moving to more complex models. The problem is one of capturing the right signals and correctly weighting them. Things are constantly changing."

Capturing a state of continuous change with the consequent need for continuous adaptation, as described by Lo (2004), is a key challenge in financial modeling. The use of cross-sectional data might be an answer insofar as it allows the researcher to capture stable relationships verified on a very large number of cases. In fact, cross-sectional data might include thousands of variables per cross-section multiplied by hundreds of data points. Another possible approach might be the use of double-tier models, one of which is a simple model and the other, a meta-model that drives the simple model's parameters. GARCH models, stochastic volatility models, and regime-shifting models are well-known examples of double-tier modeling.

Sample Biases. Survivorship biases—indeed, sample biases generally—are traps that modelers must be aware of and avoid to the greatest extent possible because, as noted by Samuelson (1994), we have only one historical sample and it is of bounded size. Any backtest is prone to the problem of look-ahead biases because many ideas have probably been tested on the same data sample.

To understand the dangers of survivorship bias, consider the following experiment. Construct a sample consisting of all stocks that belonged to the S&P 500 Index at least once in the past, say, 10 years. Now, consider a simple strategy that consists of going long the stocks with the highest average prices on a moving window of three months and going short the stocks with the lowest average prices in the same time window. With this simple strategy, which does not, per se, include any data snooping, one obtains very high in-sample returns. These attractive returns are biased, however, because we cannot know at any moment what stocks will be in the S&P 500 at a future date and disappear in any out-of-sample test.

As one investment consultant remarked with reference to management searches, "We look closely at the statistical inference techniques used and, in particular, at how the problem of survivorship biases is dealt with."

Selecting, Building, and Backtesting Models

As noted previously, financial models are methodologies for reasoning about data and are guided by finance theory and statistical analysis with the objective of identifying overvalued and undervalued stocks. As one participant observed, quants are problem solvers. So, what model choices do quants have?

A leading investment consultant said, "The model selection process must be sensible. There must be a reason why a factor is generating returns. It must make economic sense and must be tested in tests that are statistically honest. Factors must be truly orthogonal and should show stability—that is, stable beta loadings—over time."

Orthogonal factors are independent, or at least uncorrelated, which means that knowledge about one factor does not imply knowledge about the other factors. Orthogonality is a tricky concept. If we consider only correlations, factors can be mathematically made orthogonal, creating new factors that are portfolios (linear combinations) of old factors. If one orthogonalizes factors in this way, however, the economic meaning of new factors may not be transparent.

The requirement for orthogonality and economic transparency can be difficult to meet or, at least, may call for a difficult process of interpretation. In addition, orthogonality means that stocks are uncorrelated when we are using *same-time correlation*, but other correlations—for example, cross-autocorrelations—may play an even more important role than pure same-time correlation.[21]

The economic reasoning used in the model-building phase differs according to the type of model, fundamental or technical, the manager has selected. *Fundamental* models work on fundamental data, such as balance sheet items and Wall Street analysts' estimates of future returns. *Technical* models work on "technical" data, such as the behavior of time series of prices, returns, trading volumes, and external data (e.g., interest rates). Models that use fundamental data tend to capture the evolution of company fundamentals and then derive pricing information; models that use technical data model prices or returns directly without making any evaluation of a company.

One source said, "In our multifactor quantitative model, there is a focus on fundamental factors. These account for 90 percent of the factors in our approach; technical factors account for the remaining 10 percent of the factors." Another source said, "Most of our models are fundamental, although some of the new stuff is technical."

---

[21]Cross-autocorrelation is the correlation of one time series with a time-shifted (lagged or led) version of a second time series.

The availability of low-cost high-performance computers and of powerful econometric software has enabled a new generation of models that mimic the work of the traditional fundamental manager. A quantitative manager can now sit down with a fundamental analyst or a fundamental manager and build a model that translates their fundamental reasoning into a model. Only a few years ago, doing so would have been much more difficult because it would have involved the programming of basic econometric functions, which are now available in off-the-shelf software.

We asked survey participants how they managed the model-building and backtesting processes. **Figure 4.2** indicates that one-fourth of the participants said that their firms allowed several processes. In this type of question, participants were asked to check all the appropriate boxes; the figure shows the total responses. At 65 percent of the participants' firms (20 of 31 participating firms), quantitative models are built and backtested by the asset manager; at about 39 percent, quantitative models are built and backtested by the firm's central research center. The rest practice variations on these processes.

Various explanations were cited for the choice of model-building and backtesting processes. The explanations were typically tied to the firm's origins or to how the firm acquired and now manages its quantitative business. A source at a firm in which asset managers build and backtest their own models remarked, "Our organization was formed over the years, through acquisitions. More recently, we put together a quant organization, which is itself decentralized, as elements were brought in from outside. Each quant manager is responsible for his or her own

Figure 4.2. Methods of Managing the Model-Building and Backtesting Process

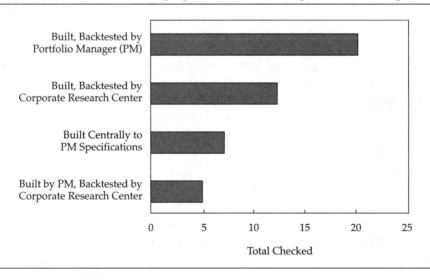

models." Another source from a firm with a disciplined quantitative business grown in-house said, "Our central research center models for the investment teams. Each model has to go through a technical committee and an investment committee to ensure that it is not cannibalizing an existing strategy."

A slight trend among survey participants is to put model implementation and model backtesting at the corporate research center, although in many cases, the models will be built to the specifications of the asset manager.

Sources also cited a coming together of quantitative research and portfolio management. This merging is certainly already the case at some of the largest quantitative houses, those that began in the passive quantitative arena, in which, as one source put it, "The portfolio manager has Unix programming skills as a second nature."

Model Updating

The need to continuously update models was identified by sources as one of the major challenges to a quantitative investment process. A consultant to the industry remarked, "The specifics of which model each manager uses is not so important as long as management has a process to ensure that the model is always current, that the model is relevant as a prism for looking at the universe, that it is not missing anything. One problem in the United States in the 1980s and 1990s was that models produced spectacular results for short periods of time and, then, results decayed. The math behind the models was static, simplistic, and able to capture only one trend. Today, quants have learned their lesson; they are paranoid about the need to do constant evaluation to understand what is working this year and might not work next year. The problem is one of capturing the right signals and correctly weighting them when things are constantly changing."

The need to sustain an ongoing effort in research was cited by investment consultants as a key determinant in manager choices. One consultant said, "When quant performance decays, it is often because the manager has grown complacent. And then, things stop working. When we look at a quant manager, we ask: Can the manager continue doing research?"

One way to ensure that models adapt to the changing environment is to use adaptive modeling techniques. One quantitative manager said, "You cannot use one situation, one dataset in perpetuity. For consistently good performance, you need new strategies, new factors. We use various processes in our organization, including regime-shifting adaptive models. The adaptive model draws factors from a pool and selects variables that change over time."

The use of adaptive models and strategies that can self-adapt to changing market conditions is an important research topic. An adaptive model is a model that automatically adapts to market conditions. An example is a clustering algorithm, which forms clusters of similar stocks as a function of market conditions.

From a mathematical point of view, many tools can be used to adapt models. Among the adaptive models is a class of well-known models with hidden variables, including state-space models, hidden Markov models, and regime-shifting models. These models have one or more variables that represent various market conditions. The key challenge is estimation: The ability to identify regime shifts sufficiently early requires a rich regime structure, but estimating a rich regime-shifting model requires a very large data sample—something we rarely have in finance.

From Measuring Quantities to Fully Automated Processes

By the term "fully automated investment process," we mean a process in which return-forecasting models are linked to an optimization model with risk tolerance profiles fed to the optimizer to construct a portfolio. It refers to the automation of one fund in its daily operations. There are also other decisions to be made; an example is determining the capacity of the fund.

With reference to an automated process, an investment consultant remarked, "The entire process has to be complete, from the data scrubbing and return-forecasting model selection and backtesting to tying the forecasting model to a risk estimation model, either third party or in-house, to incorporate risk covariance. Then, there must be the ability to estimate the transaction cost impact, and lastly, the optimizer, which should separate alpha from systemic risk."

We asked survey participants whether they thought quantitatively driven equity investment processes were moving toward full automation. Interestingly, as **Figure 4.3** shows, participants were divided almost evenly in their responses, but fully 24 percent were undecided.

Industry observers and consultants also had difficulty identifying any trend related to full automation. One source remarked, "There are all degrees of automation among quants, and we see no obvious trend either toward or away from automation."

The early screening or scoring systems that firms used produced lists of stocks that constrained a manager's choices in portfolio construction. These models, typically based on fundamental data, produced forecasts of a restricted universe of stock returns in an attempt to find mispricings that might represent a profit opportunity, without considering risk. This type of process might or might not be automated, in the sense that, at this level of portfolio complexity, human managers can realistically construct portfolios themselves.

Today's models can produce forecasts of returns and estimates of risk. These models work in a global sense: Risk and return are computed for members of an entire investable universe—for example, all stocks in the Russell 1000 Index. A universe of 1,000 stocks has 499,500 individual correlations, so the number of correlations alone requires models that make the correlation estimation process robust. A screening

Figure 4.3. Responses to: Most Quant-Driven Equity Investment Processes Are Moving toward Full Automation

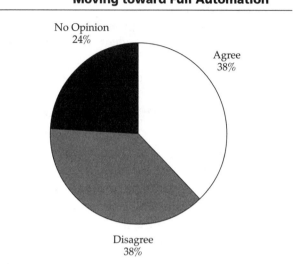

system might explore the same Russell 1000 universe, but the output would be a simpler set of information. Actually, a firm might use a hierarchy of models that, first, produces a tactical asset allocation model and, then, constructs portfolios.

No unassisted human can reasonably be expected to construct portfolios made up of hundreds of stocks and assign a weight to each stock. Constructing large diversified portfolios calls for an automated procedure. The optimizer can assign weights to implement the optimal risk–return trade-off as a function of the investor's risk profile.

Obstacles to full automation are not the result of technical shortcomings. There are presently no missing links in the automation chain going from forecasting to optimization. Full automation is doable, but successful implementation of it depends on the ability of a firm to link a return-forecasting tool seamlessly with a portfolio formation strategy. Portfolio formation strategies might take the form of full optimization or might be based on some heuristics with constraints.

Progress toward full automation will ultimately depend on performance and investor acceptance. Consultants whom we talked to for this study were divided in their evaluation of the advisability of full automation. One source said, "All things being equal, I actually prefer a fully automated process once you believe that a model is stable and effective over a long time." In a divergent view, another consultant said, "I am not keen on fully automated processes. I like to see human intervention."

5. Performance Issues

In this chapter, we take a look at what sources had to say about how quantitative products have been performing recently, and we then consider the performance of quantitative funds during the events of July–August 2007. Next, we discuss the strategies that sources might implement to improve performance. And finally, we turn to the implications of past and current performance for the future of "quant" processes and products.

Are Quants as a Group Outperforming?

When we studied equity portfolio modeling two years ago (Fabozzi, Focardi, and Jonas 2007), quantitative managers were excited about the strategies' performance. When we started asking the same question in the beginning of 2007, much of that excitement was gone. And when we asked it in July and August of 2007, we were greeted with a lot of head shaking.

According to data on fund performance released by Lipper at the beginning of 2008, the year 2007 was indeed not a good one for quantitative managers. As **Table 5.1** shows, Lipper data, which separate the performance of quantitative and nonquantitative managers into four categories, show that quantitative funds under-performed in 2007 in all categories except market neutral. This outcome is a significant inversion from 2005, when quantitative managers were outperforming nonquantitative managers by a comfortable margin in all four categories, and from 2006, when the Lipper data show them still outperforming in all categories except enhanced index funds. Note, however, that the Lipper data are neither risk adjusted nor fee adjusted.

A source at a large financial firm with both fundamental and quantitative processes explained, "The problem with the performance of quant funds is that there was rotation in the marketplace. Most quants have a strong value bias, so they do better in a value market. The 1998–99 period was not so good for quants because it was a growth market; in 2001–2005, we had a value market, so value-tilted styles such as the quants were doing very well. In 2006, we were back to a growth market. In addition, in 2007, spreads compressed. The edge quants had has eroded."

A study by Casey, Quirk & Associates (2005) examined the performance of quant products over the 2002–04 period—a time that overlapped a value market cycle—and found that quantitative active U.S. large-cap equity products outperformed other active U.S. large-cap equity products by 103 bps a year over the three-year period

Table 5.1. Fund Flows and Performance of Quantitative and Nonquantitative Funds: 2005–07 by Year

Fund Type	Total Assets 31/Dec/07 (millions)	Fund Count	Established Net Flow (millions)			Average Total Return		
			31/Dec/04 to 31/Dec/05	31/Dec/05 to 31/Dec/06	31/Dec/06 to 31/Dec/07	31/Dec/04 to 31/Dec/05	31/Dec/05 to 31/Dec/06	31/Dec/06 to 31/Dec/07
Large-cap equity ex quantitative funds	$1,272,662.50	2,060	−$44,180.60	−$31,475.20	−$48,262.60	5.78%	12.10%	7.82%
Quantitative funds ex large-cap equity funds	50,339.30	577	4,920.90	7,190.50	2,147.10	10.37	13.70	4.23
Enhanced index funds ex quantitative funds	13,762.10	154	−694.70	−228.20	2,186.40	5.61	14.78	5.70
Quantitative funds ex enhanced index funds	62,829.50	642	3,990.00	6,377.00	2,193.10	8.59	13.33	4.86
Equity market-neutral funds ex quantitative funds	6,297.80	45	302.60	2,233.40	884.40	2.29	5.35	4.69
Quantitative funds ex equity market-neutral funds	62,188.50	635	4,146.30	6,161.40	1,908.80	9.67	13.55	4.76
Long-short equity funds ex quantitative funds	11,593.90	92	1,204.80	2,881.10	3,910.40	6.56	11.37	6.10
Quantitative funds ex long-short equity funds	62,533.50	616	4,138.10	6,328.40	2,073.70	9.64	13.44	4.77

Source: Lipper.

ending 31 December 2004.[22] The study found outperformance most pronounced (120 bps) in the large-cap value segment and least pronounced (70 bps) in the large-cap growth segment. The outperformance of quantitative managers reportedly narrowed in 2005 but widened again in 2006. Unfortunately, no update covering the recent growth market cycle was available at the time this book went to print.

The question is: If markets are cyclical with respect to style returns, can we expect quant outperformance to be only cyclical? A leading investment consultant remarked, "What is most successful in terms of producing returns—quant or fundamental—is highly contextual: There is no best process, quant or fundamental. I hate to say it, but any manager—quant or fundamental—has to have the wind at his back favoring the factors."

Speaking in August 2007, the head of active quantitative research at a large international firm said, "It has been challenging since the beginning of the year. The problem is that fundamental quants are stressing some quality, be it value or growth, but at the beginning of the year, there was a lot of activity of hedge funds— much junk value, much froth. In addition, there was a lot of value–growth style rotation, which is typical when there is macro insecurity and interest rates go up and down. The growth factor is better when interest rates are down; the value factor is better when rates are up. Fundamental quants could not get a consistent exposure to factors they wanted to be exposed to." Another source said, "We try to be value– growth balanced, but the biggest danger is rotation risk. One needs a longer term view to get through market cycles." The chief investment officer of equities at a large asset management firm added, "Growth and value markets are cyclical, and it is hard to get the timing right."

The problem of style (value versus growth) rotation is part of the global problem of adapting models to changing market conditions. Value versus growth represents one factor, and it is captured in three-factor and four-factor models of equity returns, such as the Fama–French (1993) model. But many more factors could be at work (e.g., see Alford, Jones, Lim, and Litterman 2004). So, factor rotation is more than simply a question of value and growth markets because other factors, such as momentum, are subject to the same seesaw. One side of the factor prevails in one market situation but then loses importance and is replaced by its opposite or some other factor in other market conditions.

From a modeling perspective, the problem with factor rotation is that it is difficult for models to capture the change in the relative importance of factors. Often, models are estimated as linear regressions on factors, and these regressions cannot capture the change in factors early in a rotation. As mentioned in Chapter 4, hidden

---

[22]The research universe in the study included 32 quantitative managers managing 70 products with total assets of $157 billion and 387 "other" managers managing 688 products with total assets of $925 billion.

variables may be used to represent the "state of the market" with factor loadings changing as a function of the market state. Models with hidden variables are difficult to implement because they require very long data samples (see the appendix, "Factor Models"). If hidden variables are not used, an alternative solution is to estimate models on a moving window.

Other reasons have been cited to explain why the performance of quantitative products as a group has been down since the 2006–07 period. Among them is the increased number of quantitative managers using the same data, using similar models, and implementing similar strategies. A source at a firm that uses both quant and fundamental processes said, "Why is performance down? One reason is that many more people are using quant today than three or five years ago. Ten years ago, the obstacles to entry were higher: Data were more difficult to obtain; models were proprietary. Now, we have third-party suppliers of data feeds, analytics, and backtesting capability."

A consultant concurred. Speaking in mid-2007, he said, "The next 12 to 24 months will be tough for quants for several reasons. One problem is the low volatility, but another problem for quants is the ease with which people can now buy and manipulate data. The problem is that too many people are running similar models, so performance decays and it becomes hard to stay ahead. Performance is a genuine concern."

Another source said, "Quant performance depends on cycles and the secular trend, but success breeds its own problems. By some estimates, $4 trillion is under quantitative equity management if we include index funds, long-only active funds, hedge funds, and proprietary desks. There is a downside to the success of quants. Because quants have been so successful, if a proprietary desk or a hedge fund needs to get out of a risk they can't get out of, it leads to a liquidity sell-off. So, you get trampled on as others have more to sell than you have to buy. The business is more erratic because of the sheer size and needs of proprietary desks and hedge funds whose clients have 6- to 12-month holding periods, as against six *years* for traditional asset managers."

Not all sources agreed that performance is suffering because quantitative managers are using the same data and/or similar models. One source said, "Although all quants use the same data sources, I believe that there is a difference in models and in signals. There are details behind the signals and in how you put them together. Portfolio construction is a very big thing."

Another source added, "All quants use similar data, but even minor differences can lead to nontrivial changes in valuation. If you have 15 pieces of information, different sums are not trivial. Plus, if you combine small differences in analytics and optimization, the end result can be large differences. There is not one metric but many metrics, and all are noisy."

Risk-Adjusted Performance. In the post-Markowitz age, performance must be adjusted for the risk incurred. Although this requirement is now almost universally accepted in the investment management community, its meaning is subject to various interpretations, and its application is not straightforward. To see the counterintuitive aspects of "risk adjusting" performance, consider the following.

According to finance theory, markets exhibit a risk–return trade-off. So, the first question about correcting performance for risk is: Should we use the actual risk–return trade-off of the market or some (more or less) arbitrarily constructed measure?

Suppose we adopt the first view. In the world of the capital asset pricing model, the risk–return trade-off is easy to ascertain. In practice, however, return distributions are not normal and we have no reason to believe that the risk–return trade-off is, by any measure, constant over time. The risk–return trade-off of an investor is typically represented as a utility function. We can, theoretically, define a utility function for the entire market, but it is practically impossible to determine its exact shape. Therefore, we cannot determine the exact risk–return trade-off of a financial market. We must use approximations, such as the variance of returns, or concepts such as the exposure to factors. But these measures come from a complex modeling exercise: We measure the performance of one model or strategy by using the uncertain results of another model! In addition, these approximations may be totally at odds with the reality of extreme events. The events of July–August 2007 demonstrated that extreme events do exist when strategies are highly leveraged.

In practice, we use performance measures that are a compromise between arbitrariness and uncertainty. For example, we may measure risk through exposures to a given set of factors. But how, knowing that factor rotations occur and that capturing these rotations is difficult, do we evaluate these exposures?

The implication of these considerations is that anything related to performance is uncertain by nature. When we adjust for risk, we choose a measure of risk even though we know (1) there are dimensions of risk that we are ignoring and (2) the objective risk–return profile of the market is time varying so we are probably applying a correction that is not in line with the market.

Asset managers speak of alphas and betas as if they were permanent objects. But as everybody knows, they are not (see the box titled "Alphas and Betas: The Whole Story?"). Understanding whether an alpha is a true alpha or a beta in disguise is a modeling exercise in itself. In addition, the market may be truly nonlinear, which would make any statement about alphas and betas a first-order approximation at best.

Nevertheless, asset managers must measure performance on a risk-adjusted basis. Recall from Chapter 3 that *tighter risk control* was rated by survey respondents as the most important consideration in their firm's decision to adopt a quantitative equity investment process. Given the discussion here, how have quantitative products been performing on a risk-adjusted basis?

Alphas and Betas: The Whole Story?

Alphas and betas are the two main concepts used to analyze fund performance. The problem with these measures is that they are usually examined in a static, crystallized view of markets. In a dynamic view of markets, alphas and betas are time-varying quantities subject to uncertainty.

Empirically, we find that all returns are highly correlated. The returns of any active long-only strategy will have a portion that is correlated with market returns and a portion that is not. Long–short portfolios might be able to hedge their exposure to markets, but in general, active strategies will be at least weakly correlated with the markets.

To quantify the performance of an investment strategy, we assume a linear relationship between the return of the fund in excess of the risk-free rate, r_f, and the returns of a number of factors:

$$r_f = \alpha_f + \beta_{f1} r_{f1} + \ldots + \beta_{fK} r_{fK} + \varepsilon,$$

where

$\quad r_{fj}$ = returns of various factors
$\quad \beta_{fj}$ = factor loadings
$\quad \alpha_f$ = excess idiosyncratic return of the fund
$\quad \varepsilon$ = noise term

There are many betas, one for each of the factors we want to assume as benchmarks (Anson 2008).

As the remuneration for risk, betas are a double-edged sword. A higher beta means a higher expected return, but it also means greater fluctuation in asset values. A positive alpha, however, is always desirable. A positive alpha means that a fund earns an expected return in excess of factor returns. (Regardless of factor returns, a positive alpha does not imply, of course, that a fund is earning a return that is a positive number in an absolute sense; both market and fund returns can be negative.) A fund with a zero market beta is called a "market-neutral fund." The expected return of this type of fund (in excess of the riskless rate) is uncorrelated with the market benchmark and consists of "pure alpha" (which, please note, can be positive or negative). In practice, these pure alphas are not necessarily independent of market conditions at large; usually, the returns of a market-neutral fund will be exposed to other factors.

The two key assumptions behind the calculation of alphas and betas are (1) there is a linear relationship between the factor returns and the fund's returns and (2) this relationship is time independent. Neither of these assumptions has been verified. If we relax the assumption of linearity, then alphas and betas are, at most, first-order approximations of the true relationships. And if we relax the assumption of time invariance, then alphas and betas change over time.

Market correlations also change over time. Actually, the changing level of market correlations is captured by multivariate versions of autoregressive conditional heteroscedasticity and generalized autoregressive conditional heteroscedasticity models and stochastic (i.e., probabilistic) volatility models. The general belief among finance practitioners is that periods of high correlations are followed by periods of low correlations. As a result, the beta of any strategy is unlikely to remain constant over time. Nor is there any compelling reason to believe that alphas remain stable over time. Whatever the strategy used to produce excess returns, it depends on factors that are probably dynamic, not static.

First-order approximations such as alpha and beta might be sufficient for analyzing the performance of a traditional fund. An investor in a quantitative strategy, however, is well advised to consider alphas and betas to be stochastic quantities that are subject to (possibly large) movements. We know that in periods of financial turmoil, such as July–August 2007, a sudden rise in correlations may occur. Any rise in correlations affects betas and alphas.

The Casey, Quirk & Associates (2005) study looked at performance adjusted for risk. As **Figure 5.1** shows, this study found that the median quantitative product had a three-year tracking error vis-à-vis the benchmark of 2.7 percent compared with a tracking error of 4.5 percent for the median "other" products for a three-year period ending 31 December 2004. A co-author of the study said, "From what we have seen in examining performance of quants in the U.S. large-cap segment, they have outperformed fundamental managers when one takes into consideration the type of returns. In our study, which examined U.S. large-cap returns for the three-year period 2002–2004, the most compelling finding was that quant managers outperformed fundamental managers with half the risk. Quants as a group are better at quantifying all the risks and what is likely to go wrong."

Figure 5.1. Returns and Tracking Error: Quantitative Products vs. "Other" Products, Three-Year Period Ending 31 December 2004

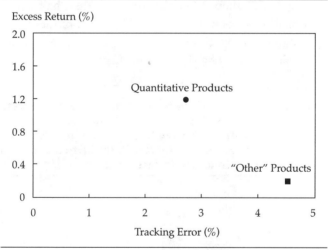

Source: Casey, Quirk & Associates (2005).

Indeed, investment consultants identified risk management as among the biggest pluses for a quantitative process. According to one source, "Quantitative managers have a much greater awareness of risk. They are attuned to risk in relation to the benchmark as well as to systemic risk. Fundamental managers are often not aware of concentrations in, for example, factors or exposure."

Similar considerations apply to sustainability of performance. If markets change, performance evaluated by any measure should also change. In evaluating the sustainability of performance, there is an element of arbitrariness if we apply the same correction in different periods.

If quantitative processes are credited with tighter risk control, they are also credited with more consistent performance. As discussed in Chapter 3, according to survey respondents, the need to *ensure more stable returns* was the second most important consideration—only slightly behind risk control—in their firm's decision to adopt a quantitative equity investment process.

A source at a large international investment consultancy said, "Past performance can never be used as a guide to the future. Nevertheless, with quant processes, there is more evidence of sustainability—more than in a fundamental process whose performance depends on an individual's judgment."

Performance vs. Efficient Markets. The question about performance of quant strategies in more efficient markets is: In such markets, will quantitative managers be able to maintain performance if profit opportunities decay?

We asked survey participants whether they believe that as market inefficiencies are exploited, quantitative managers are finding it increasingly difficult to generate excess returns. **Figure 5.2** shows that slightly more than half agreed. When we turned the question around, as in **Figure 5.3**, 74 percent of the survey participants agreed that, although profit opportunities would not disappear, quantitative managers would find it increasingly hard to exploit them.

Figure 5.2. Response to: As Market Inefficiencies Are Exploited and Disappear, Quantitative Equity Managers Are Finding It Increasingly Difficult to Generate Excess Returns

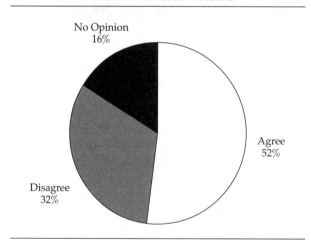

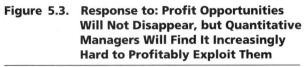

Figure 5.3. Response to: Profit Opportunities Will Not Disappear, but Quantitative Managers Will Find It Increasingly Hard to Profitably Exploit Them

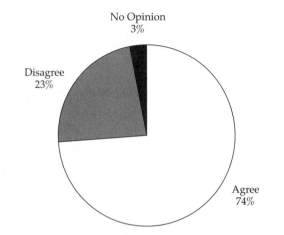

One source remarked, "Performance is getting harder to wring out, not because everyone is using the same data and similar models, but because markets are more efficient. So, we will see Sharpe ratios shrink for active returns. Managers will have to use more leverage to get returns. The problem is more acute for quant managers as all quant positions are highly correlated because they all use book-to-price return as a factor; fundamental managers, on the other hand, differ in their evaluations of future returns."

We can summarize the preceding discussion of the performance of quantitative equity funds as follows:

- Markets will continue to exhibit uncertainty; that is, we will not enter a period when forecasts become almost certain, because the interaction of a variety of strategies produces uncertainty.
- Markets will continue to exhibit a risk–return trade-off, in the sense that high returns will entail high risk.
- Finding risk strategies with a risk–return trade-off that is particularly attractive will become increasingly difficult.

Performance in Specific Market Segments

Quantitative equity management started in the U.S. large-cap market segment, but it has been extended to all equity markets. As one source said, "Any area once open only to fundamental managers is now open to quants, including emerging markets and small cap, although these have not yet been picked over by the quants. You need data providers in there before quants can move in, and the data providers are now there with both wider and more timely market coverage."

We asked survey respondents to rate the performance of quantitative products in various equity markets. Perhaps reflecting the experience of the survey participants, they identified large-cap equity markets—U.S. followed by non-U.S.—as the equity markets in which quantitative methods perform best. Next came the small-cap/midcap segments—again, U.S. followed by non-U.S. Finally came the emerging equity markets.

Note that, in principle, large-cap equity markets should offer fewer profit opportunities than the small-cap segment because the large-cap segment is well researched and heavily traded. Quantitative managers, however, are thinking about two important considerations. First, large-cap stocks cover all industry sectors and thus offer all available diversification opportunities by industry sector. For this reason, a quantitative manager can create low-risk, low-return strategies in large-cap markets and then boost returns through leveraging. Small-cap markets, being more volatile, offer more direct profit opportunities but lend themselves less to leveraging.

To our knowledge, no studies separate the performance of funds attributable to the investment strategy itself from performance attributable to leveraging. Fama and French (1993) and similar studies indicate that more profit opportunities exist in the small-cap segment, although these findings have been challenged. The returns of small-cap stocks versus large-cap stocks are not the only element responsible for the difference in returns of strategies used in the large-cap segment versus the small-cap segment. We need to consider the entire spectrum of available factors, not only size, and their relative performance in various markets. Academic studies exist that do so for some factors.[23]

We asked survey participants to evaluate performance trends in each market segment. According to participants, evidence of performance decay is strongest in the U.S. large-cap segment. Consultants shared this evaluation. Among the causes for the decay in performance, sources cited a greater efficiency in U.S. large-cap pricing and exposure in this segment to industrial sectors negatively affected by the subprime mortgage crisis. A source at a firm with both fundamental and quantitative processes commented, "U.S. large-cap stocks are now more efficiently priced, so there is not a great deal of value in modeling this market."

Speaking in midsummer 2007, a leading investment consultant said, "It is our observation that performance of quant funds in the large-cap equity market has been down in 2007. Some quant value buyers and managers were more exposed to industries negatively impacted by the credit problems than were fundamental managers. Also, quants are looking for an earnings-quality component that has dissipated in time."

---

[23]The interested reader can see Hou, Karolyi, and Kho (2006).

The deleveraging of many quantitative funds since July–August 2007 has probably added to a decay in performance, although the main impact here of deleveraging concerns quantitative long–short funds. Given the prevalence of leveraging in quant strategies (up to six times in some strategies), subsequent deleveraging probably also had an impact on long-only strategies.

As for performance trends of quantitative strategies in the non-U.S. large-cap segment, a segment that quant firms are now developing thanks to new disclosure rules and more analyst coverage in those markets, most survey participants reported that performance has been stable. One source said, "There is a great deal of value in modeling the non-U.S. large-cap market because not as many people are modeling this market as are modeling the U.S. large-cap market."

An industry observer remarked, "International equities are now at less of a disadvantage than they once were for quants. For example, firms in the FTSE 100 Index now follow similar disclosure rules to U.S. large-cap rules, and there is also more analyst coverage. So, it is now possible to handle international firms quantitatively. The edge a fundamental process once had in having an analyst on the ground is now less important. In the United States, the prominent quant firms have now introduced non-U.S. large-cap funds."

As for the U.S. and non-U.S. small-cap and midcap segments, evaluations of performance trends by sources were mixed. Some sources cited better performance, but others cited performance decay.

A source at a European firm with €15 billion in equities under management commented, "Quantitative funds in the small/midcap U.S. and non-U.S. markets are outperforming all our other quantitative equity funds. Small/midcap stocks are often below the radar screen of the more fundamentally managed processes."

Some consultants, however, reported performance problems in the small-cap and midcap segments. An investment consultant in the United States said, "Many quant strategies in the small-cap space have not been meeting their benchmarks. Some are off 500 bps to 1,000 bps. Our explanation is twofold: There is limited fund capacity here (too many assets have flowed into the small-cap space), and in 2007, we saw lower cross-sector volatility. Abnormal returns dissipated more quickly than expected."

Referring to problems in modeling small caps and midcaps, a consultant to the industry remarked, "Our instinct is that quant does not perform as well in the U.S. and non-U.S. small/midcap segments as in U.S. large cap. Our hypothesis is that in small cap—U.S. as well as global—fundamental managers have an advantage because of the data issue. Small-cap managers typically include some 100 securities in their portfolios, of which about 10 drive all the returns, especially the small caps with less than $1 billion in capitalization and in which management owns a significant amount of the stock. In this case, the market price does not reflect all the information required for a quant process—for example, share price, volatility, earnings forecasts—as they do not exist. In addition, these stocks do not trade a lot. Nevertheless, some firms are using quant methods in this segment. They have huge portfolios with upwards of a thousand small caps. In this way, they can spread their bets wider and better than a fundamental manager."

As for emerging markets, although data are still an issue in modeling equities, a few sources noted that, because of better reporting standards and more data, performance is improving. An investment consultant said, "We now have 10 years of data on firms in emerging markets, and corporate reporting among these firms is getting better. Companies in these markets have embraced international market standards."

Nevertheless, volatile political situations and the exposure to one-time big events make quantitative management a challenging proposition in emerging markets. A source at a large international manager commented, "Sure, there is now more data on emerging market firms, but there is more idiosyncratic firm risk."

Yet, some so-called emerging markets are now so big that working in them *without* quantitative modeling is becoming difficult.

Performance in Equity Investment Styles

We also asked survey respondents to rate the performance of quantitative management in various equity investment styles. As **Figure 5.4** reports, respondents rated a quantitative approach in active equity as performing best in the enhanced index arena, followed by 130–30-type strategies.[24] Performance in managing structured funds was rated high by all those using quantitative methods in this arena, but it scored lowest because few participants rated it. Several sources also cited the good performance of quantitative processes in tactical asset allocation and "benchmark unaware" funds.[25]

Sources remarked that quantitative managers dominate in the enhanced index arena. This state of affairs is not surprising because quantitative managers dominate the passive investment arena and are credited with tight risk control.[26] An investment consultant commented, "The only space in the active equity offerings specific to quant funds is enhanced indexation, in which the product is a 1–2 percent tracking error–type product. Quants dominate here."

---

[24]Keep in mind that this type of figure shows the total ratings survey participants gave each item.

[25]Benchmark-unaware investing, in contrast to much other active investing, does not start with the weights of each security in the benchmark and then add to or subtract from them according to the manager's security-specific views. Instead, the manager buys those securities that the manager thinks will go up the most and/or sells short those the manager thinks will go down the most.

[26]Note that even an index manager needs to know the methodologies to forecast because these methods are needed to select indices. This knowledge will become more important in the future with the diffusion of fundamental indices, which are ultimately active strategies.

Figure 5.4. Performance of a Quantitative Approach in Various Equity Investment Styles as Rated by Survey Participants

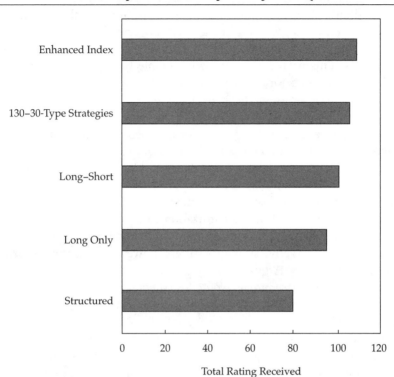

An interesting development in the area of indices is the development of style-based indices, which can be considered semiactive or semipassive. The objective of these indices is to capture the systematic biases that are supposed to be in the market. New wrinkles in style management are represented by such firms as WisdomTree and Research Affiliates, which offer "fundamentally weighted" indices for various investment universes. These products have been quite successful. Pioneered by Research Affiliates founder Robert Arnott, a quantitative manager, fundamentally weighted indices weight stocks not by market capitalization but by combinations of fundamental variables such as earnings, book value, and dividends. Other players in the style-based index arena are the traditional index providers, such as Morgan Stanley Capital International and the FTSE Group.

An investment consultant said, "Style-based indices, such as the semiactive approaches, are now playing a big role. These indices capture more good aspects of portfolio construction and allow many different strategies, such as fundamentally weighted strategies."

Some people question whether style-based indices are "real" indices, on the grounds that, theoretically, indices should reflect the market, not specific strategies, and indices should allow any number of investors to invest in them. These are not solely issues of terminology: Being at least partially actively managed, these indices suffer from problems of capacity: Only a fraction of all investors can reasonably invest in them. This problem is especially notable with fundamentally weighted style indices, but it exists for all style indices.

Style-based indices might be considered types of standardized quantitative strategies. It will be interesting to follow their development. In almost every other industrial sector, some level of standardization has been achieved. Even in the medical profession, traditionally oriented toward individual reasoning, standard protocols have developed for the treatment of many diseases. The availability of electronic data feeds, automated text handling, and computerized quantitative methods makes standardization feasible in asset management. Passive investment strategies have already brought a first level of standardization to the industry. And according to consultants, clients that have invested in passive funds have been "well served."

Standardization of active strategies suffers, however, from the problem of the *self-reflexivity* of markets. Arguably, if a large fraction of the investors were to invest in style-based indices, these indices would lose their appeal. But if such indices exist in sufficient variety, they might be able to capture some basic active opportunity present in the market.

As regards the performance of quantitative offerings in 130–30 and similar strategies, most sources give quantitative managers a (slight) advantage over fundamental managers. The abilities to solve complex problems and backtest results were cited as the factors giving quantitative managers an advantage. A source at a firm that has both fundamental and quantitative processes said, "Quant managers perform best when problem solving is called for, as in the 130–30-type strategies, or wherever there is complexity in portfolio construction." A consultant noted, "Quant and fundamental managers compete in the long–short 130–30 arena. There is evidence of slightly more success among the quant managers, as they can backtest the product." Another source was even more affirmative. According to this source, "Quant firms in the United States are absolutely positioned to dominate the market of 130–30-type strategies."

According to finance theory, 130–30 strategies should offer better performance than long-only strategies. A long-only strategy misses opportunities to profit from selling short. If forecasts could be correctly made, the advantage of the 130–30 strategies would obviously be true. But forecasts are uncertain. Globally, equity markets show positive returns, so a short sale is a bet against the market trend. Clearly, profitable shorting would require a higher level of forecasting accuracy than that required by going long only. But as one source commented, "The problem is that if we aren't good in forecasting on the long side, there is no reason to believe that we will be good in forecasting on the short side."

Long–short market-neutral strategies are a different kind of bet from 130–30 strategies. A long–short market-neutral strategy bets on the spread between high and low returns. The reasoning behind it is that the spread of returns is uncorrelated with market trends. A 130–30 fund can be thought of as the sum of a long–short market-neutral strategy and a long-only strategy. In principle, the two strategies should be uncorrelated; thus, the long–short market-neutral strategy should provide a benefit in terms of diversification. In practice, however, one discovers that in bull markets, a positive contribution from the short portion is difficult to achieve.

Conditions Affecting Performance

When asked what market conditions pose the most serious challenge to a quantitative approach in equity portfolio management, survey respondents ranked conditions as shown in **Figure 5.5**. Rising correlation ranked first; least challenging to these respondents were dissipation of earnings and nontrending markets.

Figure 5.5.   Recent Market Conditions Rated by Survey Participants in Terms of the Challenge They Pose to a Quantitative Approach

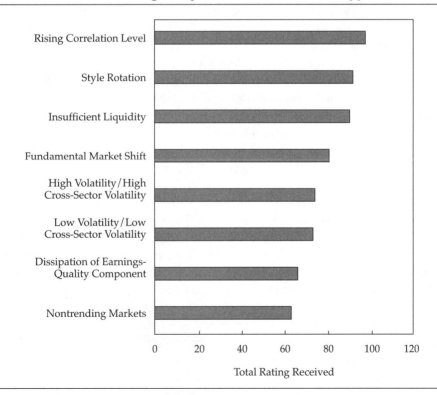

Consider the problem posed by rising correlations. As previously remarked, return-forecasting models tend to exploit reversion to a central mean. That is, models try to exploit the fact that mispricings will be corrected in the future. So, the problem is one of the interrelationship between correlations and mean reversion.

From a purely mathematical point of view, correlations and mean reversion can be independent. That is, two mean-reverting processes can be correlated, negatively correlated, or uncorrelated. Correlations might or might not be important for different types of models. What is important is the correlation level between predictive factors and returns. If a factor has predictive power, then returns are correlated with lagged values of the factors. If returns are at the same time correlated with present and lagged factors, then factors should be autocorrelated and thus predictable. On correlations, a source said, "Correlations are not a problem most of the time, but in times of stress, correlations converge."

Khandani and Lo (2007) pointed out the sharp rise in correlations over the 1998–2007 period. They observed that this rise reflected a much higher level of interdependence in financial markets. Interdependence is one of the factors responsible for the contagion from the subprime crisis to the equity markets in July–August 2007. When problems began to affect the equity markets, the liquidity crisis started. ("Liquidity" is a word that takes on different meanings in different contexts. Here, we are using it to refer to the possibility of finding buyers and thus to the possibility of deleveraging without sustaining heavy losses.) A CIO commented, "Everyone in the quant industry is using the same factors. When you need to unwind, there is no one there to take the trade: Quants are all children of Fama and French. A lot of people are using earnings revision models." Another source remarked, "Because quants have been so successful, if they need to get out of a risk—for whatever reason—they can't get out. This leads to a liquidity sell-off."

With reference to the challenges posed by a fundamental market shift, the head of quantitative management at a large European group said, "Quantitative processes remain sensitive to regime change." A consultant commented, "Quant funds tend to underperform when there is a fundamental shift in the market, when signals turn up or down, such as occurred in March 2003. I am not convinced that quants can handle a regime shift, be it with hidden Markov models or with something else. I know people who are working on this, but I believe that there is a need for a subjective override in the case of a market shift. The problem is that we live in a world that is changing perpetually, so the past might be a poor guide. If we are building, for example, hidden Markov models using 20–25 years of data or even 10 years of data, that is a problem. Things change so much quicker now because of the activity of hedge funds and the liquidity in the markets."

The discussion of regime shifts is empirical, not theoretical. In fact, the question is whether the time of a shift between regimes can or cannot be modeled. Mathematically, one can represent shifts that are highly predictable as well as shifts that are nearly random. Regimes might be highly persistent, but shifts might be difficult to detect. Alternatively, regimes might be easy to detect but not persistent, so transitions would be nearly random. In addition, each state might contain a high level of uncertainty.

Regime shifts are one way to represent nonlinearities; if one is using nonlinear models, one might not need to shift regimes. A source that is using nonlinear models said, "Fundamental market shifts do not pose a big challenge to us. Our quant process is adaptive, albeit with a lag."

With reference to the challenge posed by low volatility, a source that provides modeling for asset managers remarked, "Why has the performance of quant funds been down in the past 12–18 months? I think it is due to low volatility. There are more profits to be made with momentum strategies when volatility is high."

Another source said, however, "Too little volatility reduces the opportunity set for adding value, but otherwise, low volatility and low cross-sector volatility are not a problem. High volatility and high cross-sector volatility are more problematic. Our process tends to underperform following volatility spikes."

As mentioned, nontrending markets were not considered to pose much of a challenge. One reason may be that trends are not used because markets do not trend. A return trend is too simple to exploit in our modeling era. Note that all models, however, need the persistence of some characteristic of the market. If everything changes randomly, no forecast can be made. That axiom holds for fundamental managers and quants alike.

A consultant remarked, "Quant funds underperform in markets that don't trend, in markets without any clear pattern, or in markets characterized by rotation—for example, telecoms up for two or three days and then down and then utilities up for two or three days and then down. The problem is that the noise is too difficult to sort out."

One source using nonlinear models said, "Nontrending markets are not a challenge to us. Our quant process actually does better in nontrending markets with good breadth." The reason is that their nonlinear models have been able to capture relationships of a more stable nature than trend following.

Generally, as **Figure 5.6** indicates, survey respondents consider the major challenges to come from too many market participants using similar models and the same data. The activity of certain hedge funds was also considered to pose a serious challenge. As discussed later in this chapter, sources identified the activity of certain hedge funds as the number one factor contributing to the losses during the market turmoil of July–August 2007. These challenges merge to form another highly rated challenge—namely, the need to update models continuously.

We have already discussed the problem of too many quantitative managers using the same data and similar models and will say more on this aspect when we discuss measures that quantitative managers might use to improve performance.

Figure 5.6. General Factors Rated by Survey Participants in Terms of the Challenge They Pose to a Quantitative Approach

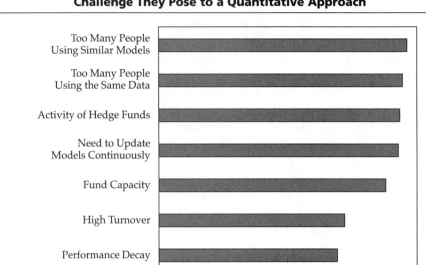

Fund capacity was also considered by survey participants to be an important challenge. The problem of understanding capacity in portfolios constructed by computers has gained much attention since the market turmoil of mid-2007, during which many quant funds suffered significant losses that have been only partially recovered since then. Investment consultants we talked to believe that capacity deserves more attention. Speaking just before the events of July–August 2007, one source said, "Most quant managers cannot effectively measure the dilution of returns related to capacity management. It should be intriguing."

In September 2007, after the disappointing performance of its quantitative market-neutral hedge fund, Goldman Sachs Asset Management wrote in its letter to investors that the problem was one of too much money in the strategy (see Cobley 2007).

Understanding capacity is a multifaceted problem. Profit opportunities are not evenly distributed; there are pockets of profitable stocks. When a fund's assets under management grow, models are forced to choose among a pool of stocks, not all of which are optimal, which causes performance decay. One might be tempted to conclude that the capacity problem is a sign that the fund strategy is not unique. Because there are only a limited number of really good opportunities, a portfolio manager who attempts to exploit them will find that the strategy becomes similar to everybody else's.

Performance and 2007 Market Turmoil

We asked survey participants to evaluate factors that contributed to the losses incurred by some quantitative equity funds in the July–August 2007 turmoil. As **Figure 5.7** shows, participants identified the unwinding of long–short positions by hedge funds as the most important factor in contributing to the losses of that summer. One source said wryly, "Everyone is blaming the quants; they should be blaming the leverage."

Figure 5.7. Factors Contributing to the Losses Incurred by Some Quantitative Equity Funds in the Summer of 2007 as Rated by Survey Participants

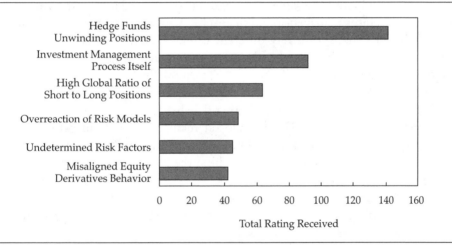

Another source explained, "Quants had a lot of positions in common with people who had to liquidate positions in July–August 2007. The principal problem was one of liquidity. A lot of leveraged managers needed to unwind things for which there was no market, to answer massive margin calls as banks got scared due to the subprime crisis. Quant managers all had similar positions, although they were massively diversified. The problem was one of the statistical arbitrage people; there was too much money in short positions in a specific period of time."

A CIO of equities who is responsible for fundamental and quant management styles added, "July to August [2007] was a dramatic departure from the normal. There was a huge unwinding of positions run on quantitative models. There was some $1.3 trillion invested in model-driven long-only (enhanced index and active) strategies and some $800 billion in hedge funds with high leverage, which gives an impact of $3 trillion. The sell-off was due to hedge funds covering their short positions and selling their long positions. The huge unwindings created a lot of correlations because many stock returns move in the same direction. Fundamental managers and quantitative managers were not equally hit; the shift in orientation of the market from value to growth is an explanation."

In a Lehman Brothers report, Rothman (2007) documented how factors inverted their behavior in the month of July 2007. Rothman attributed the poor performance of equity market-neutral managers to the fact that most factors—especially value factors—had turned perverse. For example, he noted that in July 2007, the book-to-price factor return was −3.2 percent against an average of 2 percent with a standard deviation of 2.9 percent; the trailing earnings-to-price factor return was −3.1 percent against an average of 1.8 percent with a standard deviation of 2.6 percent.

One source commented, "The market turmoil of August 2007 was truly unique. The models all looked the same. Everyone was selling and buying the same thing. Quantitative equity managers found themselves with similar exposures to value and growth but, I believe, to a very different extent. Then, there is the question of awareness of conflicting signals. My perception is that hedge funds have become more multistrategy, so in the August [2007] turmoil, they unloaded equity positions to meet margin calls."

We asked survey participants whether they believe that the investment process itself, which produced similar portfolios at many firms and failed to detect the investment risk, contributed to the losses of July–August 2007. Participants rated this the second most important factor behind the losses.

Musing on the losses of summer 2007, a research director at a plan sponsor said, "Investment management asks, 'Is this investment a good idea? Does it help maximize portfolio return per unit of portfolio risk taken?' Risk management asks, 'Do we own the assets that we think we own? Are they worth what we think they are worth? Are we being defrauded? Will our counterparties be able to pay their obligations?' So, if the crash was the result of (1) everyone having similar positions, based on value investing, with all of them being unwound at the same time or (2) technical considerations, such as selling perfectly good investments to meet liquidity needs caused by a collapse in the values of subprime mortgage–related paper, then I am defining that as an investment management question, not a risk management question. My definition would put the risk of any type of market crash into the investment management category. I realize that in some organizations, risk management is defined more broadly to include issues such as tail risk, a spike in correlation, or herd behavior, which my definition would put in the investment management category."

The similarity in strategies and in factors that can lead to liquidity problems has been discussed. As for spikes in correlation, one source in Europe commented, "The heavy shift in correlations that took place during the market turmoil of 2007 has certainly impacted the quantitative process." The increase in correlations in times of crises is well documented in financial literature. An increase in correlation means a reduction of diversification and poor performance of hedging strategies.

In analyzing the increase in correlations over the 1998–2007 period, Khandani and Lo (2007) concluded that this increase has made markets more global and also more prone to contagion. In particular, they compared the 1998 Long-Term Capital Management problem with the market turmoil of 2007. In 1998, a credit problem hit some firms hard but did not spread to other segments of the market (perhaps, partly as a result of the swift action of the authorities), whereas in 2007, a credit problem did spread to the equity markets.

Among the other factors suggested as *having contributed to* the losses, survey respondents rated them in declining order as shown in Figure 5.7. There was some apprehension that as-yet-unidentified risk factors played a role.

We asked participants whether they believed too much money was invested in long–short funds. The CIO of equities at a large asset management firm mused, "Can the markets support $3 trillion of assets managed quantitatively with multiple leverage, up to eight times? I would like to see more long-only and hedge fund regulation [to limit allowable leverage]." Another source said, "Society has to be net long on assets or we are in the Stone Age again."

Others disagreed. One source said, "I believe that it was liquidity, not net positions, that aggravated the sell-off." Note, however, that the liquidity problem, in turn, was a result of funds deleveraging and thus taking liquidity out of the market.

In *explaining* the losses, **Figure 5.8** indicates that participants attributed them to a reduction in spreads because of massive deleveraging. Other factors, such as poor model performance, were rated as significantly less important.

Improving Performance

Because the performance of many quantitative equity funds has decayed over the past year or two, we asked participants what they were likely to do to try to improve performance. **Figure 5.9** indicates that the search to identify new and/or unique factors was the most frequently cited strategy; complementary to it was the intention to use new models.

A CIO of equities said, "Through the crisis of July–August 2007, quant managers have learned which of their factors are unique and will be focusing on what is unique. There will be a drive toward using more proprietary models, doing more unique conceptual work. But it will be hard to get away from fundamental concepts: You want to hold companies that are doing well and you do not want to pay too much for them. So, you must develop unique models and be circumspect when describing what you are doing."

Figure 5.8. Factors Explaining the Losses Incurred by Some Quantitative Equity Funds in the Summer of 2007 as Rated by Survey Participants

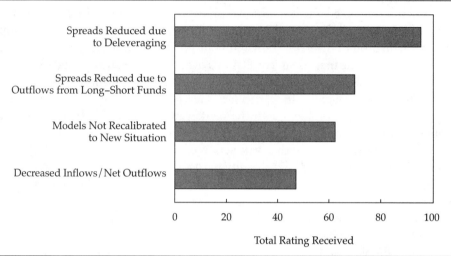

As for the need to use new models, the global head of quantitative strategies at a large financial group remarked, "Regression is the state of the art of today's tool kit. To get better performance, we will have to enlarge the tool kit and add information and dynamic and static models. People are always changing things; maybe we will be changing things just a bit quicker."

Speaking with a journalist following the market turmoil of July–August 2007, Gregg Berman of the RiskMetrics Group commented that the life span of a good trading algorithm collapsed to three to four years in the mid-1990s and has now collapsed to just two to three months (Urstadt 2007). Berman added that he expects to see the life cycle of a successful algorithm continue to drop.

The changing nature of modeling has received academic attention. John Mulvey of Princeton University has proposed a new paradigm of investment for long-term investors called "essential portfolio theory" (EPT). According to Mulvey (2005), the objective is to construct broadly diversified and leveraged portfolios that allow one to capture all the return opportunities in the market. EPT calls for dynamic, forward-looking models and optimization. Although intended for long-term investors, the EPT paradigm also reflects the reality of today's portfolio management processes for those who embrace a wholly quantitative modeling approach.

Other strategies to improve performance include attempts to diversify sources of business information and data (for example, the use of high-frequency data). As one investment consultant said, "All quant managers rely on the same set of data, but one cannot rely on the same data and have an analytical edge. It is a tough sell.

Figure 5.9. Strategies to Which Quantitative Managers Will Turn in an Effort to Improve Performance as Rated by Survey Participants

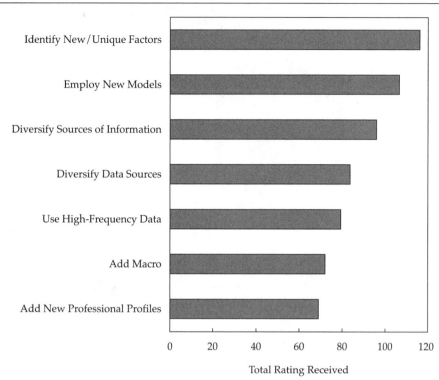

Quant managers need an informational edge, information no one else has or uses. It might be information coming out of academia or in the footnotes of balance sheets or other information in the marketplace that no one else is using."

Figure 5.10 reports that slightly more than 60 percent of the survey participants agreed that if everyone is using the same data and similar models, quantitative managers need a proprietary informational edge to outperform. Sources mentioned that some hedge fund managers now have people in-house on the phone doing proprietary market research on companies.

As for using high-frequency (up to "tick-by-tick") data, **Figure 5.11** indicates that survey participants were divided almost in thirds as to believing high-frequency data can give an informational edge, not believing it, and having no opinion. True, experience with using high-frequency data in equity portfolio management is still limited. One source remarked, "Asset managers now have more frequent updates. What was once monthly is now daily—with services such as WorldScope, Compustat, Market QA, Bloomberg, or Factset. But the use of intraday data is still limited to the trading desk."

Figure 5.10. Response to: With Everyone Using the Same Data and Similar Models, Quantitative Managers Need a Proprietary Informational Edge to Outperform

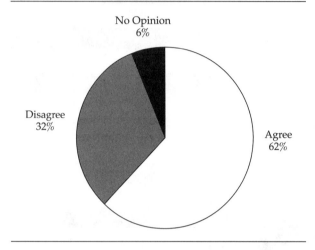

Figure 5.11. Response to: High-Frequency Data Give an Informational Edge in Equity Investment Management

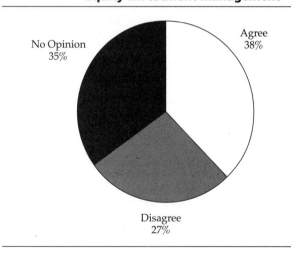

Finance theory tells us that high-frequency data improve our estimates of correlations but that they are less useful in forecasting returns. With high-frequency data, volatility and correlations become almost observable quantities. However, whether the ability to produce a highly accurate estimate of instantaneous volatility will improve returns is not clear.

The role of data in identifying unique factors was emphasized by a source at a large quantitative firm: "How do we build unique factors? We gather data ourselves as well as using third-party data."

Adding macroeconomic data was rated next to last on the list in Figure 5.9 of seven possible strategies to improve performance. Many sources mentioned that macro data are already in the price of the stock. Nevertheless, some firms are evaluating the opportunity. A source that models for asset managers remarked, "Most quant models today are bottom up. We believe that adding macro will be important and are thinking of implementing this. True, stocks can mimic the macro, but can you capture this immediately?"

Although adding new people with nontraditional professional backgrounds was the lowest rated of strategies for improving performance, some sources mentioned that in the long run, a new "people profile" would be required to give quantitative managers an informational edge. A head of active quantitative research said, "Because everyone is using the same data and models, quants will need far more detail to produce better returns going forward. The problem for quants will be how to capture information such as that in the footnotes of balance sheets, discrepancies in corporate statements, and the like. In the medium term, quants will need to connect the information, which will require people with an information systems background to scan corporate statements and reports and use such techniques as multidimensional clustering as a way to aggregate fundamental data. Now, the people profile is slanted more toward accounting and finance backgrounds."

Some sources mentioned that rather than adding new people with unorthodox backgrounds, they will be taking a look at their modeling teams, perhaps trying to find new ways of cross-fertilization of ideas. Among other strategies that participants believe will allow them to improve performance in the future are improving capacity management and liquidity management and implementing low-turnover strategies.

Performance and Net Flows

Estimates of the size of assets under management in active quant strategies vary from a few hundred million dollars to more than $1 trillion. In a study comparing cumulative net flows to U.S. large-cap quantitative strategies with the flows to "other" products in 36 months during the 2001–05 value market, Casey, Quirk & Associates (2005) found, as **Figure 5.12** shows, that assets grew by 25 percent at quantitative funds and remained almost flat for other funds. A co-author of the study commented, "What we have seen in our studies that looked at U.S. large-cap

Figure 5.12. Cumulative Net Flows as a Percentage of Total Assets for Quantitative vs. "Other" Products, 31 December 2002 to 30 June 2005

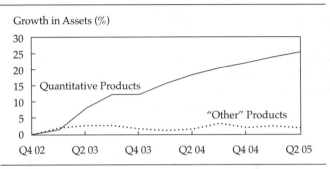

Note: Q = quarter.
Source: Casey, Quirk & Associates (2005).

funds is that since 2004, investors have withdrawn money in the U.S. large-cap segment under fundamental managers but active quants have held on to their assets or seen them go up slightly."

Addressing the question of net flows into quantitatively managed equity funds before July–August 2007, a source at a leading investment consultancy said, "There has been secular growth for quant equity funds over the past 20 or so years—first, into passive quant [index funds], and over the past 12–36 months, into active quant, given their success in the past value market. Right now, there is about an 80/20 market split between fundamental and active quant management. If active quants can continue their strong performance in a growth market, which I think we are now in, I can see the percentage shift over the next three years to 75/25, with active quant gaining a few points every year."

Despite the high-profile problems of some long–short quantitatively managed funds during the summer of 2007, 63 percent of the respondents remained optimistic that as more firms introduce quantitative products and as exchange-traded funds give the retail investor access to active quant products, quantitatively managed equity funds, in aggregate, will continue to increase their market share relative to tradition-ally managed funds. When the question was formulated as in **Figure 5.13**, however, that optimism was somewhat dampened. Figure 5.13 reports that only 42 percent of the survey participants disagreed with the statement that quantitatively managed funds would *not* be able to increase their market share in 2007 and 39 percent agreed.

Among the sources that believed quantitative funds would not increase their market share in 2007, one said, "Recent events will have a limited impact on long-only quant funds and more of an impact on 120–20-type strategies. But I expect to see slower growth in inflows to quant funds for several years."

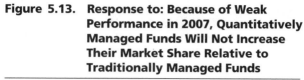

Figure 5.13. Response to: Because of Weak Performance in 2007, Quantitatively Managed Funds Will Not Increase Their Market Share Relative to Traditionally Managed Funds

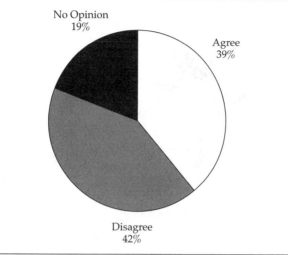

When we talked to consultants just before the July–August 2007 market turmoil, many of them were skeptical that quantitative managers could continue their strong performance. These sources cited performance problems dating back to 2006. A source at a large consultancy in the United States said, "I see no new wave of money flowing into quant funds. Flows will be consistent but not growing. Why? It is a function of client appetite—there will always be 20 percent of clients that are not comfortable with quant strategies, and in the year 2006, quants did not do so well relative to fundamental managers."

A consultant in Europe said, "Assets under quant management grew a few years ago, but now quants are only maintaining, not taking, market share from fundamental managers."

In view of this discussion, we asked survey participants if, given the poor performance of some quant funds in 2007, they thought traditional asset management firms that had diversified into quantitative management would be reexamining that commitment. **Figure 5.14** reports that nearly a third agreed but 52 percent disagreed. Those who agreed tended to come from firms in which quant equity assets under management represented less than 5 percent of all equities under management or firms with a substantial fundamental overlay to the quantitative process.

The head of quantitative equity at a large traditional manager said, "When the firm decided back in 2000 to build a quant business as a diversifier, quant was not seen as a competitor to fundamental analysis. The initial role of quant managers

Figure 5.14. Response to: Traditional Asset Managers That Have Diversified into Quantitative Management Will Be Reexamining That Commitment

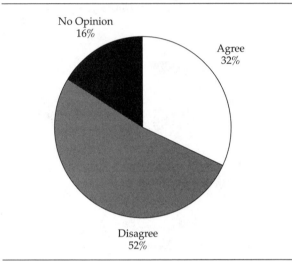

No Opinion
16%

Agree
32%

Disagree
52%

was one of being a problem solver—for 130–30-type strategies or wherever there is complexity in portfolio construction. If quant performance is down, the firm might reconsider its quant products. Should it do so, I would expect that the firm would keep on board some quants as a support to its fundamental business."

Another head of quantitative strategies at a large traditional manager said, "These are difficult times for quants. The temptation for firms with fundamental and quant management styles will be to eliminate the quants."

6. The Challenge of Risk Management

In principle, truly quantitative funds implement a risk–return optimization or quasi-optimization and, therefore, manage risk at the source. That is, risk management is embedded in the investment management process itself; the asset manager is the risk manager. Traditionally managed funds, in contrast, do not include an explicit risk–return optimization and might call for an independent risk control function. As one source at a firm with both fundamental and quantitative management styles put it, "Compared with the free-wheeling fundamental retail managers, quantitative management is a risk-managed practice with low tracking error."

Risk management may generate a conflict of models if the principles behind the return-forecasting models are not the same as those behind the risk models. Consider that risk measurement is carried out by models that are subject to the same uncertainty as forecasting models. For example, style or factor rotation affects both forecasting models and risk models. Moreover, standard risk models may be insufficient to understand the risk intrinsic in some complex fund strategies. For example, exposure to the usual risk factors is insufficient to capture the fat-tailed risk involved in some 130–30 strategies.

The head of quantitative strategies at a large international manager commented, "The question is: How do you calibrate to take risk into consideration? There is a need for dynamism, to better calibrate the factors that influence volatility. The MSCI Barra risk models did not work in the market turmoil of July–August 2007. We use various risk models, including Northfield and APT, but with the latter, you do not get the economic sense behind the statistics."[27]

We asked participants to evaluate today's risk management tools, especially in the wake of the July–August 2007 market turmoil.

Risk Measurement in Normal and Extreme Conditions

The events of July–August 2007 highlighted, for anyone who needed reminding, that quantitatively managed funds can be exposed to the risk of extreme (i.e., rare, large, and adverse) events. In explaining the losses incurred during the summer of 2007 at Goldman Sachs' flagship Global Alpha Fund (which trades bonds, currencies, and

---

[27]The formal names of firms mentioned in this quote are Morgan Stanley Capital International, Northfield Information Services, Inc., and Advanced Portfolio Technologies, which is part of SunGard.

commodities as well as equities), the firm blamed the computer models for having failed to foresee the market movements. A spokesman for the firm labeled the events of early August 2007 a "25-standard-deviation event"—that is, an event that might occur only once every 100,000 years or so.[28] Note that a 25-sigma event (assuming the computation of the number of sigmas is correct) is basically impossible in a Gaussian world, but in a fat-tailed world, it may be a risk that should be considered.

Fundamentally managed funds also are exposed to the risk of extreme events— typically of a familiar nature, such as a market crash or a large drop in value of single companies or sectors. A head of quantitative management remarked, "There are idiosyncratic risks and systemic risks. Fundamental managers take idiosyncratic risks, while the 'quants' look at the marginal moves, sometimes adding leverage."

We asked participants whether they believe that the current generation of risk models has pitfalls that do not allow one to properly anticipate such risks as those that came to pass in July–August 2007. As **Figure 6.1** reports, slightly more than two-thirds of the survey respondents answered that because today's risk models do not take into consideration global systemic risk factors, the models cannot predict events such as those of July–August 2007.

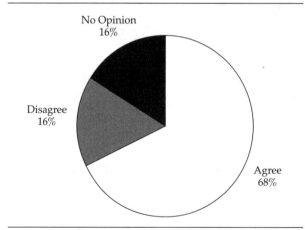

Figure 6.1. Response to: Because They Do Not Take into Consideration Global Systemic Risk Factors, Today's Risk Models Cannot Predict Severe Events, Such as Those of July–August 2007

[28]See Tett and Gangahar (2007).

One source commented, "Risk management models work only under benign conditions and are useless when needed. We use two risk methods, principal components analysis and the Six Sigma method, and two risk models, MSCI Barra and Northfield. But the risk models are misspecified, and most pairs of stocks have high correlations."

Another source responded, "There are estimation errors in everything, including risk models. We know that they will fail, so we add heuristics to our models. Risk models do not cover downside risk, but they do help control it. Studies have shown that risk models do improve the information ratio."

As mentioned in Chapter 1, whether we can expect risk models to anticipate such events as those of July–August 2007 is questionable. By definition and by construction, a risk model measures the size of *what cannot be anticipated*. Paradoxically, if the events could be anticipated, they would not be risky and a risk model should not include them. At most, a risk model should quantify the probability that events like those of July–August 2007 might happen (see the box "Can Uncertainty Be Measured?" in Chapter 2).

If this quantification is possible, the critical question then becomes: How far in advance should (and can) risk models warn of an impending deterioration of the risk situation? When should they warn that negative fat tails are waiting to hit?

These questions are somewhat academic, especially because we do not have the necessary data. For example, participants in this study (like the regulatory authorities) were unaware of both the amount of leverage that was present in the market before the turmoil of summer 2007 and the concentration. Such data would have allowed risk models to warn of impending problems.

Does Risk Control Amplify Risk?

The events of July–August 2007 have been attributed to a number of highly leveraged funds that had to deleverage to meet margin calls related to the subprime mortgage crisis. If we assume that some exogenous event triggered the massive deleveraging without a precise identification of the event, we can ask: Did risk management models make the crisis worse by forcing deleveraging that was not needed to meet margin calls? Or in general, do risk models amplify catastrophic events? When we asked survey participants what they thought, **Figure 6.2** reports that 63 percent do not believe that risk models amplify catastrophic events.

Despite the high proportion not believing that risk models amplify disaster, a CIO responsible for both fundamental and quantitative investments at a large firm remarked, "What we noticed is that, on the first big down day—Monday, 6 August 2007—the models seemed not to be working; on the second big down day, portfolios were doing poorly but the return-forecasting models were not doing so poorly. Was it due to risk controls? Fundamental managers use less risk control and are growth oriented; their portfolios suffered less." The source added, "I expect that in the turmoil following mid-2007, risk management will come under fire."

Figure 6.2. Response to: Risk Models Amplify Catastrophic Events

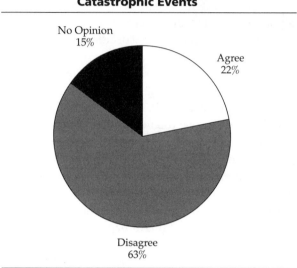

Risk Management and Derivatives

Two-thirds of the survey participants use derivatives in equity investing. When asked the motivation for using derivatives, as **Figure 6.3** indicates, survey respondents that use these securities cited derivatives' role in reducing trading costs and controlling risk.[29] Using derivatives to exploit specific market relationships was rated low. Several firms reported, however, that derivatives play an important role in efficient cash flow management.

Does the use of derivatives in equity asset management introduce new risks that are difficult to evaluate? **Figure 6.4** indicates that participants were split on the issue. **Figure 6.5** shows, however, that 63 percent of the participants believe that the use of derivatives in equity asset management entails creating parallel markets that, although in principle are related to the underlying equity prices, in practice, are driven by their own supply-and-demand schedules.

One source commented, "The derivatives markets are susceptible to chaos—they overheat—compared with normal markets. Derivatives contracts are complex, and no one knows how they will behave in various scenarios. In addition, there is credit risk/counterparty risk in dealing with entities such as Sentinel Trust Company—not a Wall Street firm—that can go up in a puff of smoke. Their going under was blamed on the subprime crisis, but it was a result of fraud."

---

[29]Recall that in this type of question, survey participants were asked to rate the various items on a scale of 1 to 5 and the figure shows the total ratings for each item.

Figure 6.3. Motivation for the Use of Derivatives as Rated by Participants

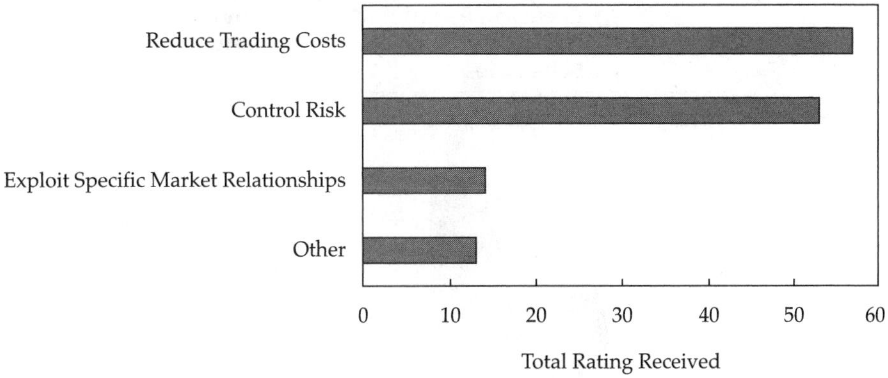

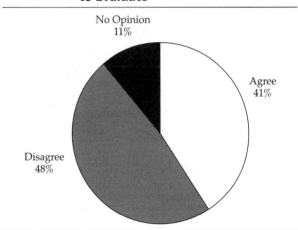

Reduce Trading Costs

Control Risk

Exploit Specific Market Relationships

Other

Total Rating Received

Note: This question was asked of only those who use derivatives.

Commenting on the July–August 2007 events, risk management professional Richard Bookstaber voiced concerns that derivatives are getting too complex and too closely interrelated; RiskMetrics' Gregg Berman shares this evaluation (Urstadt 2007) as do Khandani and Lo (2007). Derivatives are considered to have introduced a level of interdependence that is well above the level of economic correlation and that is, in addition, difficult to understand.

Figure 6.4. Response to: The Use of Derivatives in Equity Asset Management Adds New Types of Risk That Are Difficult to Evaluate

No Opinion
11%

Agree
41%

Disagree
48%

Figure 6.5. Response to: The Use of Derivatives in Equity Asset Management Entails Creating Parallel Markets Driven by Their Own Supply-and-Demand Schedules

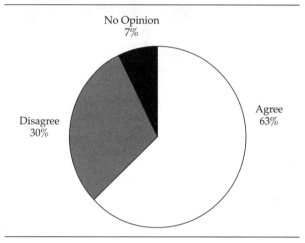

7. Summary and Concluding Thoughts on the Future

The good performance of quantitative funds in the 2001–05 period encouraged many fundamental managers to (1) add quantitative processes, such as stock-ranking systems, risk management, return attribution, and portfolio composition, and/or (2) enter the "quant" arena—by building in-house teams, buying specialized quantitative boutiques, or adding quantitative offerings to their product lines. The objective was to add the discipline of a quantitative process and diversify sources of alpha. Similarly, the relatively poor performance of many quantitative funds since 2006 has led some managers considered to be quants to take a fresh look at fundamental processes. The objective is to gain an informational edge by adding a fundamental insight on companies and thereby, again, diversify sources of alpha. Here, we summarize the findings from our survey and conversations. Then, we leave the reader with some final thoughts about the findings.

Summary of Findings

Among quantitative managers, we found no clear indication of a movement toward full automation. Although half of the survey participants believe that a movement toward full automation is occurring, the other half do not. We are likely to continue to see diversity in quantitative management that reflects the personalities and skills of each organization.

Three main objectives are behind the decision to adopt (at least partially) a quantitative equity investment process: to gain tighter risk control, to garner more stable returns, and to improve overall performance. We found the profile of a firm's founder(s) and/or the prevailing in-house culture to be correlated with the implementation of quant, in that these profiles identify whether (and how) the environment welcomes quant methods. Objectives such as improving the cost-to-revenue ratio or reducing management costs were rated low as motivating factors.

Participants in our study believe the active quantitative equity arena will continue to be characterized by the dominance of a few big players and a large number of small quant boutiques. The most important barriers to entry into the quantitative space are the firm's culture (whether fundamentally oriented firms accept quant management) and the ability to recruit people with the right skills.

Participants also believe that the best way to sell a quantitative product is to present it as an alpha-capturing opportunity. Other selling points are the enhanced investment discipline, better risk management, and the transparency of the process. Asset managers and investment consultants agreed that it is better not to mention the clever mathematics and statistics-based stock selection!

Lack of acceptance/understanding on the part of investors and lack of understanding on the part of investment consultants are considered by quantitative managers to be the major obstacles holding back investment in active quantitative equity products.

The broad diffusion of models has been credited with making markets more efficient, although some models may actually increase mispricings. Survey participants agreed that quantitative managers have been having increasing difficulty generating excess returns today because the equity markets are more efficient than in 2001–2005. Sources cited evidence of performance decay in the U.S. large-cap market as a result of greater efficiency in pricing and of exposure to industrial sectors negatively affected by the subprime mortgage crisis. Some performance decay was also noted in the small-cap/midcap sectors, but the performance of quantitative strategies was considered to be improving in non-U.S. and emerging markets thanks to better reporting standards, more analyst coverage, and more data.

Regarding performance of quantitative managers in various equity investment styles, quants were credited with market dominance in enhanced index funds and said to enjoy an advantage in the 130–30 arena. The ability of quantitative methods to solve complex problems and to backtest results were cited as the factors giving quantitative managers an advantage over fundamental managers.

Rising correlations, style rotation, and insufficient liquidity were identified as the market conditions posing the most serious challenges to quantitative approaches in equity portfolio management. In general, survey respondents consider the major challenges to come from the fact that too many market participants are using the same data and similar models. As profit opportunities are exploited, new modeling strategies must be devised. Therefore, another major challenge to quants is that models must be constantly updated.

Sources cited the unwinding of long–short positions by hedge funds as the most important factor contributing to losses at some quantitative funds during the market turmoil of July–August 2007. Interestingly, the second most important factor behind the losses is considered to be the investment management process itself, which produces similar portfolios at many firms and failed to detect the investment risk in that period.

In the drive to improve performance, the strategies most cited by quantitative managers are identifying new factors, doing conceptual work, and diversifying sources of data. The need to use new models, eventually adding dynamics—that is, models that use lagged values—was also cited. Adding high-frequency data or macro data, however, was not widely considered to provide an advantage.

Despite the recent poor performance of many quantitative funds, quantitative managers remain guardedly optimistic that they will be able to increase market share relative to fundamental managers. Investment consultants are less optimistic; they cited performance as a genuine concern.

Current risk management tools are considered to be inadequate in terms of their ability to predict severe events, such as those of July–August 2007. Although most participants do not believe that the risk models make catastrophic events worse, some sources believe that the models played a role in losses incurred by some quantitative funds in July–August 2007. For the future, respondents believe risk management systems should be able to measure such structural parameters as "connectivity" and be able to identify critical states that might lead to financial crises.

Ultimately, the challenge for quantitative managers is to extract performance (i.e., deliver stable alpha) from markets populated by large players using similar strategies. This task will call for continuous updating of strategies and models. Presently, many funds are using leverage to boost performance of low-risk, low-return funds, but the July–August 2007 events showed the dangers of using high leverage multipliers.

Concluding Thoughts

When asked to identify the future trends and challenges they see in quantitative management, survey participants cited most frequently by far the growing popularity of 130–30 types of strategies. Indeed, one industry observer qualified these strategies as "the next big thing, together with hedge funds." In theory, these strategies are a long-only fund plus a zero-capital long–short overlay. Theoretically, the advantage of this strategy is obvious: If the long–short strategy is profitable, it is a zero-cost contribution to returns with no capital invested. In practice, however, there might be two problems: (1) The strategy is leveraged, and (2) it is very sensitive to the quality of the forecasts used for shorting. One investment consultant who saw no new wave of investments into quantitative strategies in the United States said, "Quantitative managers are turning to 130–30 strategies in an effort to improve their performance, as behavioral biases have been largely arbitraged away the last two to four years. They are trying to exploit information on the short side using leverage, but that is not such a good idea."

The most frequently cited future challenge for quantitative managers is their ability to deliver stable alpha. As a roadblock to this ability, participants specifically cited overcrowding of competitors (and thus the need to differentiate their offerings in the quant arena), capacity limits, the need to identify new and unique factors and use new models to capture profit opportunities, and the ability to handle rotation and regime shifts.

The ability to deliver stable alpha is a formidable challenge for the following reason. In principle, better models should make markets more efficient and, therefore, reduce spreads in performance of the fund over the global market or benchmark. As Lo (2004) suggested, however, markets are adaptive ecologies (hence, his term "adaptive market hypothesis"). Therefore, when performance begins to decay, new investment ideas emerge to exploit the regularities created by the old strategies.

As we have demonstrated, participants view the need to continuously adapt models as one of the major challenges to quantitative managers. Following the concept of the adaptive market hypothesis, one should be able to foresee performance cycles, with old models losing profitability (perhaps with short periods of depressed performance) followed by a few good years as new strategies are devised. There is only one caveat: Markets are large but market entities are *finite*, and given the size and complexity of today's financial markets, we cannot ignore systemic issues.

We can divide systemic issues into two categories, namely, structure and size. We will start with structure.

As Khandani and Lo (2007) observed, markets have become much more interconnected than they were, say, 10 years ago, so the risk of contagion is now much higher than at the time of the Long-Term Capital Management collapse in 1998. Many market observers and participants in this study concur that the complexity of interconnections is posing a fundamental risk. Kandhani and Lo suggested that as a way to better control that risk, the industry should adopt modern mathematical tools to measure connectivity. For example, they mentioned such models as the "small world" networks studied by Watts (1999) and Watts and Strogatz (1998). Several of these models, which are based on variants of random graphs, have been proposed. In addition to the Watts–Strogatz model, the network model developed by Barabási and Albert (1999) has been applied to research in bioinformatics and computer networks. Moreover, connectivity is probably not the only structural characteristic of markets and economies that might have a bearing on financial risk.

Now consider size. The limited size of markets is a constraint that will probably gain in importance. As we have seen, the issue of capacity is becoming more important than it has been. The events of July–August 2007 demonstrated how performance decays when strategies need to reach a larger pool of stocks. For practical purposes, the capitalization of the U.S. equity market can be considered that of the Russell 3000 Index: about $13 trillion, with most of this capitalization concentrated in the top 300 stocks. *Global* market capacity also is becoming an issue. For example, the July–August 2007 events were a marketwide "liquidity crunch." That crisis thus made clear that hedge funds and their liquidity needs have an impact on global markets.

Active asset managers try to earn an excess return. The question is: How much excess return can the markets support? From the point of view of the entire economy, what is the mechanism by which excess returns are created? Is the fund management industry structured into winners and losers, with the losers providing the losses needed to support the winners? Or are markets perhaps not zero-sum games, with winners supported through the creation of money and asset inflation? Will asset managers be forced to chase larger and larger pools of assets in emerging markets, in which they will face competition from local emerging players?

In an unpublished working paper of the Courant Institute of Mathematical Sciences at New York University, Avellaneda and Besson (2005) estimated the curve of hedge fund performance degradation as a function of the size of the hedge fund market, as measured by the assets under management (AUM). Their conclusion was that an inverse relationship exists between global AUM and the performance of hedge funds. The paper estimated, albeit with many caveats, that when the AUM of hedge funds reaches $2 trillion, their returns will be equivalent to the S&P 500 Index return.

Will active managers have to deal with global issues? Yes, the likelihood is that active managers will need to consider global issues quite attentively—issues of structure and, in particular, contagion, liquidity, and correlation. Measurements of these phenomena are likely to be incorporated in the risk control systems of some firms. One question is, however, whether active managers will begin to exercise self-restraint in asset gathering as they reach capacity. There, the natural selection of the adaptive market hypothesis is likely to play a role.

Appendix. Factor Models

Factor models are ubiquitous in financial modeling. Despite their popularity and apparent simplicity, factor models have important conceptual subtleties. Among them are the following:

- Factor models of returns may be *predictive* or *nonpredictive*; that is, the same returns can be *forecasted* or *explained* by different factor models.
- Factors may be observed variables or hidden variables.
- Arbitrage considerations apply differently to predictive and nonpredictive models.
- Some of the fundamental variables involved in factors are also idiosyncratic predictors; that is, we can regress the returns of each stock on its own predictors.

In everyday language, we use the term "factor" to indicate something that has a causal link to an event. We apply the term factor to both characteristics of various events and to identifiable exogenous events. For example, we say that advertising is a factor in success— meaning that a big advertising budget contributes to the success of a product. In this case, "advertising" is the factor and the advertising budget is a characteristic that varies from company to company. But we might also say that the number of days of rain is a factor affecting crop yields at a farm. In this case, the number of days of rain is an exogenous factor that affects yields; it is not a characteristic of a given farm.

We also have a notion of hidden factors, albeit in some intuitive and imprecise way. For example, we might say, "Her strength of will was the crucial factor in her success." We mean that a mental disposition played a crucial role, although we cannot directly observe mental dispositions.

Factors are causes of events but not necessarily the common causes of many events. The commonality of causes is central, however, to the statistical, scientific notion of factors. In financial modeling, the term "factor" indicates a variable that is the common explanation of *many* variables. In particular, a factor model of returns is a parsimonious explanation of a large cross-section of returns in terms of a small number of factors.

Consider linear factor models of returns. Mathematically, a linear factor model of returns is written as follows:

$$r_i - r = \alpha_i + \sum_{j=1}^{K} \beta_{ij} f_j + \varepsilon_i, \tag{Model 1}$$

©2008, The Research Foundation of CFA Institute

where

> r = risk-free rate
>
> r_i = return of the ith stock
>
> α_i = (constant) average excess return (above that predicted or explained by the factors) of the ith stock
>
> β_{ij} = proportionality constant of the ith stock's return and the jth factor (the factor loading)
>
> f_j = return of the jth factor
>
> ε_i = noise term for the ith stock

Written as in Model 1, a factor model is a static (or, better, *atemporal*) model. There are no implicit dynamics in this model. It does not describe a stochastic (i.e., probabilistic) process; it is a representation of a multivariate random vector. Returns, factors, and noise are all random variables and thus subject to uncertainty. The factor model establishes a linear relationship between these variables.

We can think of Model 1 as the relationship between returns and factors in a given time period. Different periods should be regarded as different samples extracted from the same distribution. For each sample (i.e., each period), the realization of the K factors are K numbers. All returns of that period are various weighted averages of these numbers.

We can also write a factor model with an explicit dependence on time as follows:

$$r_{i,t} - r = \alpha_i + \sum_{j=1}^{K} \beta_{ij} f_{j,t} + \varepsilon_{i,t}, \qquad \text{(Model 2)}$$

where the addition of t to the subscripts means at time t. So, written in this form, a linear factor model states that there is the same linear relationship between factors and returns *in each moment.*

Conceptually, there is a big difference between the two formulations of a factor model. Model 1 is a relationship between random variables; Model 2 is a multiple regression of the time series of returns on the time series of factors.

In the case of Model 2, we have only one sample of the factor model because we have only one sample of any financial time series. The realization of the factors is the realized path of the factor processes (i.e., a set of sequences of numbers). If we assume that returns are independent and identically distributed variables, then the two models are equivalent. If not, Model 2 is dynamic and there may be no way to establish equivalence between Model 1 and Model 2.

Indeterminacy and Factor Rotation

A usual saying is that, without restrictions, factor models are void of empirical content. This saying may be counterintuitive because a factor model seems to establish a relationship between factors and returns. What is meant is that given any set of returns and any set of proposed factors, without restrictions, a factor model always holds. In fact, without restrictions, the factor model simply defines the residuals. That is, we can always add a random variable to another random variable and we can always add a time series to another time series.

Some might object by stating that if the time series of returns and factors are given, we can test Model 2 as an empirical multiple regression without the need to put restrictions in place. But this assertion is not true: A linear regression can be tested only if we place restrictions on the residuals. Without restrictions on the residuals, a linear regression is, as is any other model, simply a formula that defines the residuals.

What restrictions can be applied? A *strict factor model* requires that the residuals be mutually uncorrelated and also be uncorrelated with the factors. Note that this condition applies to Model 1 because it is a relationship between random variables. It is a strong constraint, generally not met by real-life returns for any reasonable number of factors. Weaker conditions that define approximate factor models have been proposed. Roughly speaking (the exact definitions are quite technical), an *approximate factor model* allows a small amount of correlation between the residuals, and if Model 2 applies, it allows for some autocorrelation of the residuals.

These restrictions are empirically important, but they are not sufficient for determining factors. The reason is that factors appear in the model only combined with betas, so any independent linear combination of these factors is empirically indistinguishable from the original factors. A matrix notation makes this aspect easy to see.

In matrix notation, a factor model is written as

$$\mathbf{r} = \boldsymbol{\alpha} + \boldsymbol{\beta}\mathbf{f} + \boldsymbol{\epsilon}, \tag{3}$$

where

$\mathbf{r}$ = n-dimensional vector (hereafter, "n-vector") of excess returns

$\boldsymbol{\alpha}$ = n-vector of constant means of returns

$\boldsymbol{\beta}$ = $n \times k$ matrix of loadings

$\mathbf{f}$ = k-vector of factors

$\boldsymbol{\epsilon}$ = n-vector of residuals

Given any nonsingular, square $K \times K$ matrix $\mathbf{A}$, we can write

$$\mathbf{r} = \boldsymbol{\alpha} + (\boldsymbol{\beta}\mathbf{A}')(\mathbf{A}\mathbf{f}) + \boldsymbol{\epsilon}. \tag{4}$$

From this expression, we can see that if we choose new factors $\mathbf{f}^* = \mathbf{A}\mathbf{f}$ and replace the betas with $\boldsymbol{\beta}^* = \boldsymbol{\beta}\mathbf{A}'$, we have a perfectly equivalent model. As a consequence, we can always "rotate" factors. That is, we can always form independent linear combinations of factors (i.e., multiply factors by a nonsingular matrix) so that they are uncorrelated and have unit variance (are *orthonormal factors*). Orthonormal factors are called "standard factors."

Again, this representation is counterintuitive. We might imagine there is something "objective" in factor models—in particular, in Model 2, in which returns are regressed on observed time series. Under the assumptions of factor models, however, factors can always be transformed into uncorrelated unit-variance variables or, in Model 2, into uncorrelated standard random walks. An important consequence is that if the model is a strict factor model, we can write the covariance matrix of returns, $\mathbf{C}$, as

$$\mathbf{C} = \boldsymbol{\beta}\boldsymbol{\beta}' + \mathbf{V}, \tag{5}$$

where $\mathbf{V}$ is the diagonal matrix of variances of residuals and $\boldsymbol{\beta}$s are the factor loadings. Equation 5 is indeed a parsimonious representation of the covariance matrix. The standardized factors, however, might be difficult or impossible to interpret.

Fundamental, Macroeconomic, and Statistical Factor Models

Of the three basic types of factor models proposed for use in financial modeling, only statistical factor models are the result of factor analysis; the other two are multiple linear regressions on regressors determined by theoretical considerations.

Macroeconomic Models. A good place to start is macroeconomic models, which are typically used in a top-down approach to asset management. Macroeconomic factor models assume that stock returns are influenced by macroeconomic variables. The variables might be interest rates, inflation, variables related to the business cycle, and so on. The assumption is that returns are a weighted sum (a linear combination) of changes in the selected macroeconomic variables. Note that macroeconomic variables are generally directly observable time series. Macroeconomic factor models are estimated by making a regression of each time series of returns on the multiple series of factors (i.e., changes of macro variables). In macroeconomic models, returns and factors are given time series; model estimation yields the alphas and the betas.

Clearly, many technical (and not so technical) issues are involved in estimating macroeconomic models. Stationarity, autocorrelations, and cross-autocorrelations of the series of factors and returns are important points to consider. The overall scheme, however, is easy to grasp: The assumptions are that factors are observable macroeconomic time series and that returns can be explained as regressions on these observed factors. Deciding what factors to include is critical. Many selections have been proposed in the literature, and many additional selections are used in proprietary models.

Fundamental Models. The second family of factor models, fundamental factor models, are typically used in bottom-up approaches to asset management. Fundamental factor models are based on the empirical observation that returns are a function of the fundamental parameters of a company—in particular, the company's financial ratios, such as, for example, the price-to-earnings ratio (P/E). Suppose that a set of fundamental parameters has been selected. At any given moment, we have a set of observations that includes each stock return and the associated characteristics that can be observed. For example, we have for each company at each moment an observation of its stock return and an observation of its P/E.

A natural question that occurs with factor models is whether changes in the characteristic of a stock (e.g., its P/E) do, indeed, affect the stock's returns. This question can be answered by, for example, performing a linear regression of historical returns on the characteristic historically (e.g., historical P/Es). Many studies have been devoted to ascertaining whether financial ratios have predictive power. Some analysts claim that ratios do have predictive power (see Campbell and Thompson 2005); others caution that this predictive power might be illusory (see Goyal and Welch 2004). In practice, asset managers probably adopt proprietary methods that are more complex than a simple linear regression, but the fundamental idea is to exploit the sensitivity of a stock's returns to changes in the fundamentals of the stock.

Consider that neither the P/E nor any other characteristic is, in itself, a factor. A *factor* is a time series—one number for each moment for the entire market. At each moment, we have a characteristic value for each company. We expect that the P/E affects returns; thus, we expect to be able to write a function that represents the (approximately fixed) relationship between returns and the P/E. Yet, in a factor model, we want to find a factor that is *common to the entire market* in such a way that the returns of each company are affected by that factor multiplied by a beta that is company specific.

To understand the explanatory or predictive power of ratios, we should consider the ratio of each company in relation to the ratios of all other companies. The reason is that average ratios change over time. A ratio for a given company that is high relative to that of other companies in one period could be low relative to other companies in another period without the ratio itself changing. So, we must somehow normalize the ratios to some market average.

An even more fundamental point is the question of whether ratios are true characteristics of a company or represent a company's sensitivity to some factor that is common to all companies.

How do modelers go from characteristics to factor models? Given that they have the P/E of each company, what value do they assign to, say, the P/E common factor? The answer is not obvious. The theoretical answer, initially proposed by Rosenberg (1974), is the following: We fix the model so that the model parameters, the alphas and the betas, are functions of the characteristics, and we estimate factors from the returns and the parameters.

Perhaps this theoretical approach can be better understood in the simplest fundamental models, the country/industry models, in which characteristics are country and industry affiliation. In a country/industry model, the β_{ij} terms are constrained to be 1 when stock i belongs to industry j and to be 0 otherwise. Factors are estimated by regressing returns on the betas.

Macroeconomic factors are observed, but characteristics-based factors are hidden factors recovered through a mathematical process. Chamberlain and Rothschild (1983) demonstrated that in a large market (mathematically, in an infinite market), factors can be approximately mimicked by portfolios (exactly mimicked in an infinite economy). Subsequently, Fama and French (1993) proposed a two-stage method for approximately mimicking fundamental factors. Their method proved to be very influential in academia and in the practice of finance.

To illustrate the Fama–French methodology, we will consider only one feature— the P/E.[30] In the first stage, we rank all stocks as a function of the P/E and then construct two fractile portfolios using those stocks in the highest fractile and the lowest fractile of the feature—in our example, the highest and lowest fractile of P/E multiples. The corresponding factor return for that period is the difference between the average returns of the highest and lowest fractiles. The procedure is repeated for each feature. In the second stage, we regress returns on the factors thus constructed. Many firms now use Fama–French types of factors but perhaps with a selection of features that differs from those originally proposed.

Statistical Models. The last family of factor models we will discuss is the statistical factor models. Statistical factor models do not make any economic assumption about how factors are generated. They simply assume that returns can be represented by a factor structure, be it strict or approximate, with appropriate restrictions. Many technicalities are involved in estimating a statistical factor model, but a variety of techniques can be used, including factor analysis and principal components analysis. Note that in statistical factor models, only returns are observed; factors and betas are estimated.

Misspecification. Given the proliferation of models, and in view of the fact that linear factor models can be used both to explain and to predict, an important question is: How many different models of the same returns can be correctly specified? If a strict factor structure could be correctly specified, in the imaginary case of an infinitely large economy, the answer is: only one model. More precisely, there is only one family of equivalent factor models, where equivalent means that factors in one model can be recovered as a linear combination of factors in any other model in that family of models. If we relax some of the assumptions and accept an *approximate* factor structure, many technical considerations must be made but, in

---

[30]Fama and French originally proposed two characteristics, value and growth.

general, the answer is that a family of equivalent factors can be determined, again in the limit of an infinite economy. The meaning of this statement is that, for example, macroeconomic factors might be proxied by time-varying *not* macroeconomic factors determined by statistical analysis. In practice, this statement means that in a very large market, all economic factors that affect returns can be recovered from stock returns.

Suppose, however, that a factor model is correctly specified but that we are considering only a subset of the global market—for example, U.S. stocks. In this case, we might not be able to recover all factors from returns only. Thus, we can see that the requirement of an infinitely large economy is not a mathematical subtlety; it reflects the fact that we can hope to capture all possible common influences only with a huge number of stocks.

In practice, factor models are always misspecified. In addition to autocorrelations and cross-autocorrelations of returns, factors, and residuals, we face in practice regime shifts, heteroscedasticities (i.e., volatility clustering), and many other nonlinearities. Therefore, it is unlikely that the factors of linear factor models can be uniquely determined by returns. As a consequence, different factor models might provide different insights into explaining returns. At the same time, differences among models are likely to capture nonlinearities and true deviations from a strict factor structure.

Risk Models and Predictive Models. Given the preceding considerations, we will now discuss how linear factor models can be used in both explaining and predicting returns. We say that a model *explains* returns when factors are considered at the same time as returns. Essentially, this definition means that the covariance structure of returns can be determined as a function of a small number of factors. For this reason, models that explain are considered to be risk models because they explain the exposure of returns to various risk factors.

If a factor model is used to *forecast* returns, these forecasts can be made in various ways depending on whether or not we can forecast factors or use lagged factors (i.e., if returns at time t can be explained by factors known at time $t-1$). On the one hand, if we assume that factors can be forecasted, then factor models become different mathematical structures known as "dynamic factor models." These models—essentially state space models—are rarely used in practice (see Fabozzi, Focardi, and Kolm 2006).

On the other hand, the use of lagged factors is common. In fact, it is one of the workhorses of financial modeling.

How can risk factors and predictive factors coexist? Two points of view should be considered: mathematical and financial. From a *mathematical* point of view, given a set of returns and in the absence of a well-specified strict (or even approximate) factor structure, there might be different (generally misspecified) approximate factor models. Given the many approximations and misspecifications, nothing in the mathematics of factor models precludes some of these variables being known at time t and others known at time $t - 1$.

Clearly, relationships exist between factors. Consider the family of approximate factors that explain a universe of returns. If some of them are known at time t and others are known at time $t - 1$, factors must be somehow predictable. In fact, if Factor 1 predicts returns, albeit in a probabilistic sense, and returns approximately determine Factor 2, Factor 1 must somehow predict Factor 2. This relationship has been verified empirically. Not only factors exhibit autocorrelations, so do even randomly chosen portfolios.

Consider predictability now from a *financial* point of view. In the one-factor capital asset pricing model, which is a risk model, not a predictive model, alphas must be zero. The presence of nonzero alphas would be a sign of market inefficiency, and if many securities had nonzero alphas in a large economy, arbitrage might be possible. In multifactor models, the same considerations apply. Alphas are a sign of market inefficiency, and to avoid arbitrage, only a small number of alphas can be nonzero. Therefore, in a risk factor model, the question of market efficiency revolves around the existence of alphas because markets are not forecastable.

In a predictive model, if one can forecast market returns, one does not need an alpha to earn an excess return. In this case, the questions of market efficiency and the risk–return trade-off available in the market become complex. For example, the subject of debate for a long time was whether the predictions apparently made possible by the Fama–French factors are a sign of market inefficiency, remuneration for risk, or an artifact.

Summary

Why use factor models to make predictions? Why should predictors be common to an entire market? Why can we not use idiosyncratic predictors? For example, why can we not simply try to predict returns from financial ratios instead of going through the process of creating factors? Even a predictive factor model makes predictions as a function of the sensitivity of a company's returns to common factors and ignores the idiosyncratic changes.

No definitive answers to these questions are available. Many asset managers actually try to use predictors rather than factors, although the terminology is not clear. They might use models to mimic the investment process of fundamental managers; that is, they might try to find automatically those configurations of fundamental characteristics that a human asset manager would use to make profitable predictions. Managers still need to compare predictions, however, and assess risk. So, ultimately, idiosyncratic predictions must be combined with a factor model.

Factor models are not intended to capture idiosyncratic predictability. Consider, for example, momentum. A momentum strategy is highly individualistic, in the sense that it selects those stocks that have had particularly high or low returns in some past time window. A company might experience momentum for various reasons—for example, because it has launched a new product that seems to be doing better than the initial assessment of analysts, so it keeps winning investors. Assessing this trait is very different from assessing how sensitive a company is to a global momentum factor, which ultimately reveals how much momentum there is in the market. The global momentum might be the result of, for example, a general increase in leverage by hedge funds. Asset managers that use factor models to make predictions are often those managers who need to construct large global portfolios. Constructing large global portfolios requires, to achieve diversification, capturing those effects that are shared by many companies. Idiosyncratic predictions would lead to small high-risk portfolios.

References

Alford, Andrew, Robert C. Jones, Terence Lim, and Robert Litterman. 2004. "Fundamentals Drive Alpha." *Quantitative Equity Research Notes.* Goldman Sachs Asset Management (April).

Anson, Mark J.P. 2008. "The Beta Continuum." *Journal of Portfolio Management,* vol. 34, no. 2 (Winter):53–64.

Avellaneda, Marco, and Paul Besson. 2005. "Hedge-Funds: How Big Is Big?" Working paper, Courant Institute of Mathematical Sciences, New York University (www.math.nyu.edu/faculty/avellane/HFCapacity.pdf).

Barabási, Albert-László, and Réka Albert. 1999. "Emergence of Scaling in Random Networks." *Science,* vol. 286, no. 5439 (15 October):509–512.

Black, Fischer, and Myron Scholes. 1973. "The Pricing of Options and Corporate Liabilities." *Journal of Political Economy,* vol. 81, no. 3:637–654.

Campbell, John Y., and Samuel B. Thompson. 2005. "Predicting the Equity Premium Out of Sample: Can Anything Beat the Historical Average?" Harvard Institute of Economic Research Working Paper 2084 (http://ideas.repec.org/p/fth/harver/2084.html).

Casey, Quirk & Associates. 2005. "The Geeks Shall Inherit the Earth? Quantitative Managers' Recent Edge." *Research Insight* (November): www.caseyquirk.com/docs/research_insight/05.11_RI_Geeks.pdf.

Chamberlain, Gary, and Michael Rothschild. 1983. "Arbitrage, Factor Structure, and Mean–Variance Analysis in Large Asset Markets." *Econometrica,* vol. 51, no. 5 (September):1281–1304.

Cobley, Mark. 2007. "Volatile Markets Give Quants a Rough Ride." *Financial News* (19 December).

Credit Suisse. 2007. "Quantitative Research: A Disciplined Approach." Equity Research Quantitative Analysis.

Dellaert, Frank. 2002. "The Expectation Maximization Algorithm." Technical Report GIT-GVU-02-20, Georgia Institute of Technology (February): www.cc.gatech.edu/~dellaert/em-paper.pdf.

Dempster, Arthur P., Nan Laird, and Donald B. Rubin. 1977. "Maximum Likelihood from Incomplete Data via the EM Algorithm." *Journal of the Royal Statistical Society.* Series B (Methodological), vol. 39, no. 1:1–38.

Duffie, Darrell. 2001. *Dynamic Asset Pricing Theory.* 3rd ed. Princeton, NJ: Princeton University Press.

Fabozzi, Frank J., Sergio M. Focardi, and Caroline L. Jonas. 2007. "Trends in Quantitative Equity Management: Survey Results." *Quantitative Finance*, vol. 7, no. 2 (February):115–122.

Fabozzi, Frank J., Sergio M. Focardi, and Petter Kolm. 2006. *Financial Modeling of the Equity Market: From CAPM to Cointegration.* Hoboken, NJ: John Wiley & Sons.

Fama, Eugene F., and Kenneth R. French. 1993. "Common Risk Factors in the Returns on Stocks and Bonds." *Journal of Financial Economics*, vol. 33, no. 1 (February):3–56.

Figelman, Ilya. 2007. "Stock Return Momentum and Reversal." *Journal of Portfolio Management*, vol. 34, no. 1 (Fall):51–69.

Goyal, Amit, and Ivo Welch. 2004. "A Comprehensive Look at the Empirical Performance of Equity Premium Prediction." NBER Working Paper 10483 (May): http://papers.nber.org/papers/w10483.

Grinold, Richard C., and Ronald N. Kahn. 2000. *Active Portfolio Management.* 2nd ed. New York: McGraw-Hill.

Hou, Kewei, G. Andrew Karolyi, and Bong Chan Kho. 2006. "What Factors Drive Global Stock Returns?" Working paper, Ohio State University (May): www.cob.ohio-state.edu/fin/dice/papers/2006/2006-9.pdf.

Hübner, Georges. 2007. "How Do Performance Measures Perform?" *Journal of Portfolio Management*, vol. 33, no. 4 (Summer):64–74.

Hutchinson, James M., Andrew W. Lo, and Tomaso Poggio. 1994. "A Nonparametric Approach to Pricing and Hedging Derivative Securities via Learning Networks." *Journal of Finance*, vol. 49, no. 3 (July):851–889.

Hwang, Soosung, and Alexandre Rubesam. 2007. "The Disappearance of Momentum." Working paper, Cass Business School, City University London (March): http://ssrn.com/abstract=968176.

Khandani, Amir E., and Andrew W. Lo. 2007. "What Happened to the Quants in August 2007?" Working paper, MIT (4 November): http://ssrn.com/abstract=1015987.

Knight, Frank H. 1921. *Risk, Uncertainty, and Profit.* Boston: Hart, Schaffner & Marx; Houghton Mifflin Company (www.econlib.org/LIBRARY/Knight/knrup.html).

Kurz, Mordecai. 1994. "On the Structure and Diversity of Rational Beliefs." *Economic Theory*, vol. 4, no. 6 (November):877–900.

LeRoy, Stephen F. 1989. "Efficient Capital Markets and Martingales." *Journal of Economic Literature*, vol. 27, no. 4 (December):1583–1621.

Lewis, Michael. 2003. *Moneyball: The Art of Winning an Unfair Game.* New York: W.W. Norton.

Lo, Andrew W. 2004. "The Adaptive Markets Hypothesis." *Journal of Portfolio Management*, 30th anniversary issue:15–29.

Magill, Michael, and Martine Quinzii. 1996. *The Theory of Incomplete Markets.* Cambridge, MA: MIT Press.

Minsky, Hyman P. 1986. *Stabilizing an Unstable Economy: A Twentieth Century Fund Report.* New Haven, CT: Yale University Press.

Mulvey, John M. 2005. "Essential Portfolio Theory." White Paper, Rydex Investments (May): www.rydexfundsfp.com/pdf/whitepaper_EPT.pdf.

Rachev, Svetlozar T., Christian Menn, and Frank J. Fabozzi. 2005. *Fat-Tailed and Skewed Asset Return Distributions: Implications for Risk Management, Portfolio Selection, and Option Pricing.* Hoboken, NJ: John Wiley & Sons.

Rosenberg, Barr. 1974. "Extra-Market Components of Covariance in Security Returns." *Journal of Financial and Quantitative Analysis*, vol. 9, no. 2 (March):263–274.

Rothman, Matthew. 2007. "U.S. Equity Quantitative Strategies: Turbulent Times in Quant Land." *Equity Research.* Lehman Brothers (9 August): www.dealbreaker.com/images/pdf/quant.pdf.

Samuelson, Paul A. 1994. "The Long-Term Case for Equities." *Journal of Portfolio Management*, vol. 2, no. 1 (Fall):15–24.

Tett, Gillian, and Anuj Gangahar. 2007. "System Error." *Financial Times*, North American Edition (15 August).

Urstadt, Bryant. 2007. "The Blow-Up." *Technology Review*. MIT (November/December).

Waldrop, M. Mitchell. 1992. *Complexity: The Emerging Science at the Edge of Order and Chaos*. New York: Touchstone/Simon & Schuster.

Watts, Duncan. 1999. *Small Worlds: The Dynamics of Networks between Order and Randomness*. Princeton, NJ: Princeton University Press.

Watts, Duncan, and Steven H. Strogatz. 1998. "Collective Dynamics of 'Small-World' Networks." *Nature*, vol. 393 (June):440–442.